CASEY WATSON

SUNDAY TIMES BESTSELLING AUTHOR

HARPER
element

HarperElement
An imprint of HarperCollins*Publishers*
1 London Bridge Street
London SE1 9GF

www.harpercollins.co.uk

First published by HarperElement 2020

1 3 5 7 9 10 8 6 4 2

© Casey Watson 2020

Casey Watson asserts the moral right to
be identified as the author of this work

A catalogue record of this book is
available from the British Library

PB ISBN 978-0-00-837557-7
EB ISBN 978-0-00-837558-4

Printed and bound in Great Britain by
CPI Group (UK) Ltd., Croydon

MIX
Paper from
responsible sources
FSC™ C007454

Dedicated to my wonderful, supportive family and to all of my fellow foster carers out there. To these earth angels I say, keep on keeping on, you're doing a great job, and even in those darkest moments I know that you will find something to smile about.

Acknowledgements

As always I need to thank my fabulous agent, Andrew Lownie, and the wonderful team at HarperCollins. We have two team members now, too. Our lovely new editor, Kelly Ellis, who has been so patient with us and such joy to work with (even when work at the coal face got in the way of meeting deadlines, Kelly gave me the precious time I needed in my real life, so thank you ever so much) and Georgina Atsiaris, who has been equally patient, waiting for me to find moments to read the proofs. Again, thanks! And no thanks would be complete without my eternal gratitude to my friend and mentor, Lynne – who also has the patience of a saint!

Chapter 1

'You okay, love?' I asked Mike, as the motorway spooled out ahead of us. He'd been silent for some time now. A good twenty minutes. I knew why, too. He was feeling the same way as I was. It was something we'd come to learn was an inevitable part of fostering, and which we'd come over the years to refer to as 'happy-sad'. Mostly sad, but at the same time knowing we should, and would, be happy; the strange, bittersweet feeling we both often got when we'd just said goodbye to a child. Sad that they had left us, but happy that they were moving on to a safe, loving home.

We were both happy-sad twice over in this case, our most recent placement having been a sibling one. We'd spent a month now looking after four-year-old twins called Annie and Oscar, who we had just dropped off exactly where they were meant to be. The best place. Back with their loving parents, in a new home.

1

Mike glanced across at me and smiled. 'I will be. What about you? Bearing up?'

I smiled back at him. 'I will be too. Though I'm going to miss them *big* time. I hope their mum keeps her promise and allows us the odd visit.'

'As if she wouldn't,' Mike pointed out, and he was, I knew, right, because Annie and Oscar were obviously not our usual kind of placement, having not spent their early years suffering from any kind of abuse or neglect. And not usual because during the time they spent with us, we took them to visit their mum and dad almost every single day, in hospital, where both were patients, after a horrendous house fire that had been caused by an electrical fault. They'd rescued their children – both of them, miraculously, unharmed – but had both suffered severe and widespread burns. It was our proximity to a dedicated burns unit as much as the fact that we were between placements that made us so well suited to the job.

Which hadn't really felt like any kind of job. Far from it. Yes, the little ones were distressed and bewildered in the beginning, obviously, but we'd soon settled them into a reassuring rhythm, anchored by those daily visits to see Mummy and Daddy, and the knowledge that soon they'd be properly reunited.

Needless to say, it wasn't just 'Aunty Casey' and 'Uncle Mike' who'd become besotted with them, either. They were so easy to love, and the entire family duly did. My mum and dad, especially, as just after Annie and Oscar had come to us, Dad had suffered a nasty fall and been unable to drive, which meant me spending a lot of time shuttling back and forth between our houses, with the little ones in tow of necessity. Mum and Dad were usually sanguine about these kinds of partings – they were usually the ones always telling me to buck up – but this time it was me having to hand round the Kleenex, because the pair of them were crying like babies.

But say goodbye we must, and we were all buoyed by the uncomplicated 'happy ending' – which in our line of work was never a given. So I knew we'd shake the blues off in no time. In the meantime, Mike's stomach was already moving on.

'I'm starving,' he declared. 'And in need of a large coffee. Shall we pull into the next services and grab some lunch?'

It had been a long drive – the family came from an area many miles away from the specialist burns unit – and I too was desperate for a coffee. Mostly because I'd forgone a cup earlier in the interests of not further irritating a bladder that was irritable most of the time anyway these days. The menopause, I'd been finding out, had a *lot* to answer for. Hot flushes, cold sweats, and now logistics too; as soon as I arrived in any public place these days, the first thing I did was always scope out the loos.

So I headed straight into the ladies while Mike joined the queue at the café, and it was there – not the most professionally well-appointed of environments – that I saw a text come in from my rather grandly titled 'supervising social worker' or, in old money, my link worker, Christine Bolton.

She wanted me to call her as soon as I was able, so my obvious first thought was that we'd forgotten to pack something that belonged to the twins, but running through a mental checklist, I was sure that we hadn't. The next thought – equally obvious – was that she had another child for us, but I brushed that aside too, because there was no way it would be that. It had only been hours, after all, since we'd signed off on Annie and Oscar. No supervising social worker could want that much blood out of a stone, could they? Plus, she knew we had a lot on the family plate anyway, with a new Watson grandchild on the way.

'She'll be just checking in,' Mike suggested when I joined him in the queue and wondered aloud what she could want to speak to me about. 'Asking how it all went, and so on. Tell you what, here's a good idea, Case. Why don't you phone and *ask* her?'

With no tea towel immediately to hand, I couldn't flick him with one. 'That's exactly what I was *about* to do,' I huffed, and duly did so.

Even Christine's soft, relaxed Liverpool accent couldn't disguise the urgency in her voice. 'Casey, you're going to have a few choice words for me,' she guessed correctly. 'I mean, I imagine you've not even had time to strip the beds yet, but—'

'Seriously?' I asked, re-visiting my thoughts on blood and stones. 'We're not even back home yet. You need us to take someone else? Like right now, *tonight*?'

Mike stared, open-mouthed, eyebrows arched up into his hairline.

'I'm so, so sorry,' Christine said, 'and you know I would never ask if there had been absolutely anybody else.' Hmm, I thought, where had I heard that before? Was the ghost of John Fulshaw (very much alive but no longer my colleague) wafting around somewhere in the motorway services? 'But, Casey, we are stuck, and I must tell you that this is no ordinary request. It's a definite twenty-eight-day placement.'

The emphasis was very much on the 'definite', I noted. I pursed my lips. I was becoming increasingly familiar with twenty-eight-day placements and I wasn't at all sure that I agreed with the increasing regularity of them, almost as if they were a must-have fashion trend. There was a place for them of course, and they were ideal in certain situations, such as when parents phoned social services and demanded that their children be taken into care immediately, or they would be out on the streets. The twenty-eight-day placement gave the local authority the opportunity to look deeper into the dynamics of the family situation and then decide whether to seek a care order, or to put the children back with the family, opting for putting home-based support in place instead.

Because the option existed, however – and here was where the 'increasing regularity' part came in – it was very easy for some social workers, in our ever more financially strapped service, to ask a carer to accept a twenty-eight-day placement, for no other reason than that they were struggling to find the right foster family to take them and that precious month gave them an extra month of wriggle room. (Not that the term 'wriggle room' was ever used, obviously. You couldn't have a term for something that 'didn't happen', after all.)

One thing I did know, however, was that this wouldn't be a case of that. I knew Christine felt the same way as I did about the way such orders were increasingly being 'repurposed'. So, there would have to be a good reason and she quickly provided it. It turned out that a thirteen-year-old girl called Harley was, even as we spoke, waiting in the day room of a mental health facility, for someone – anyone, it seemed – to go and collect her, as her time there was done and her bed was sorely needed by someone else.

'And she can't go back to her family,' Christine explained, 'because they can't keep her safe. And when I say "family",' she added, 'I use the term loosely, as I'm not sure there's much of one. Before Harley was sectioned under the mental health act, she'd been living with her mother, a Kayleigh Brown, who has problems of her own. There's also an older sister, Millie, but she left home just under a year ago, and is no longer in contact. It appears her leaving was the catalyst for Harley's emotional deterioration.'

'So, she was sectioned?' I asked. 'What exactly did she do?'

'From the paperwork I've been sent,' Christine continued, 'it seems that after a self-harming episode was discovered, she made several suicide attempts and had been told she could no longer attend school – they were worried for her safety and felt they couldn't police her sufficiently there – and then six weeks ago a member of the public found her about to leap from a bridge above a busy motorway. Thankfully, they were able to grab her and restrain her until police arrived. That's when she was sectioned. Because it was apparently a very genuine attempt; not just a "cry for help" type scenario. She's been in the same hospital getting treatment ever since. Though I have to tell you,' she added, in a tone that suggested she wished she could skim over it, 'they say they have done all they can for her, as she doesn't have a defined mental health issue.'

'So they're not saying she's better?'

'Not quite that, no. Maybe more that she's bet-*ter*. Which I appreciate is not the same thing, 'but they've obviously made progress. And now she's coming out of an institution and able to see her mum again and so on, well, it sounds positive at least, doesn't it? And I'm sure great strides can be made now ...'

I could tell that Mike was frustrated hearing only one side of this two-way conversation but given the nature of the call, I could hardly put my phone on loudspeaker in the middle of a service station restaurant. Instead I told Christine I needed a little while to discuss it with him first. 'As I said, we still have quite a drive before we even

7

get home from dropping the twins off,' I told her. 'But I do see the urgency. Fifteen minutes, I promise. We'll discuss it in the car.'

'I am so, so, sorry,' Christine said. 'I feel terrible dumping all this on you two right now. But, look, please rest assured that I can promise you this. Whatever the decision, this isn't one of those times where we would ask you to extend. It's twenty-eight days and that's that. End of. The mother is on board with it, and is happy to accept some intervention work during the time we have, and wants her daughter back home just as soon as she feels confident that she can keep her safe. Which is not how she feels right now, obviously.'

'Twenty-eight days, fifteen minutes – this is beginning to sound like the plot of a disaster movie,' Mike observed, as we finally sat down to eat our lunch.

He had a point too, because just as I was running through the details of what Christine had told me, so my mind was running through the plot of a different story altogether. What if the mother decided she *couldn't* keep her daughter safe at the end of those twenty-eight days? Christine had already said that Harley was determined to end her life; that it wasn't a cry for help. She had also hinted that the mother had her own difficulties of some kind, and I wished I'd asked her to elaborate on what they were. What if social services deemed her unfit to have her daughter back? There were a lot of uncertainties around this and I knew that at any minute Mike was going to point out something I was already acutely aware of.

'What about Kieron and Lauren?' he said. And there it was. Our daughter-in law, Lauren, was heavily pregnant with her and our son Kieron's second child, and we had both agreed – no, *promised* – not to take a new child on around the time the baby was due to be born, even as an emergency measure. We were effectively 'on annual leave' for a couple of weeks and that had been tacitly agreed by everyone. We had an exact date too – Mother Nature notwithstanding – a booked-in Caesarean section, various risk factors having been taken into account.

Our help was non-negotiable too. Set in stone. As Lauren's family lived too far away to be able to help out with the practicalities, I had promised that I would be around to look after Dee Dee (our beautiful granddaughter) for the first week or so and to be on hand while they settled into their new routine. And also because Kieron, although he was such a fabulous dad to Dee Dee, still had his challenges, related to his Asperger's, which included his anxieties about change. And this was, of course, going to be a big change. Perhaps not as big as becoming parents to Dee Dee, but still, it was back to newborn-baby stage, which could challenge the most calm, relaxed and stoic of people, none of which my lovely son generally was.

'I've thought about that,' I said, because I had. Had counted it up even as I'd been speaking. 'We're okay on that score. The dates will work out. Twenty-eight days with this new girl, then we'll have a couple of weeks' break until the baby comes. Don't worry about that,

Mike,' I said, even though my own doubts were already niggling. 'I'll just have to make it absolutely clear to Christine that it can't be extended under any circumstances. That after the four weeks, we are no longer available. *Nada. Non. Niet.* Come hell or high water.'

'What about on the other score, Case? The one where you say all that but when it comes to it …' He looked at me pointedly. 'Come on, you know what you're like.'

'And you know what you're like as well,' I pointed out. Because the bottom line was that *someone* had to take this poor kid on and to turn her down on the basis that we wouldn't have sufficient about us to stick to our guns about the deadline would be, well, pretty pathetic. Plus, I knew if we said no we'd both feel pretty bad. Whether she was crying for it or otherwise, this girl clearly needed help.

'Okay,' Mike said, 'and you say this poor thing is actually right now sitting in a waiting room, waiting to hear where she's going next?'

I nodded sadly. 'It's bloody awful, isn't it? The psychologists have obviously decided she doesn't have a mental health issue and she's all good to go. Just like that. She must be so scared, poor thing. Imagine being in hospital for six weeks, then being told you can't go home to your mum because she isn't ready for you. Can you imagine? Bloody awful.'

So that was us decided. Once we'd finished our sandwiches (cheese and pickle, also apparently well-travelled), we popped the lids back on our coffees and headed back outside to the car, so I could call Christine back in relative privacy.

Where, again, she made all the right noises. And I could tell she meant every word she said as she promised that she understood the non-negotiable nature of our commitment to Kieron and Lauren, and would have a plan B in place to be effective from day twenty-eight, just in case.

'Much as I hate the idea,' she added, 'I will even have another twenty-eight-day placement set up to run on straight afterwards, just in case of a worst-case scenario – you know, if Mum doesn't come through, or isn't considered up to it. It will just give us a chance to do some more work with her if need be. I will be very clear with the looked-after children team that this will happen and the care plan will reflect this. If the mother says no to a return, or even if the girl refuses to return, you and Mike don't have to worry about it. At *all*. I absolutely promise. I know how much it means to you both to take that time off with the newest member of the family, and that's exactly what you'll do, rest assured.'

'You mentioned the mother having problems of her own, Christine,' I prompted, 'I don't suppose you know what they are, do you? I mean, if it's bad, then mightn't it have contributed to the daughter's problems?'

Christine was silent for a moment. 'Sorry, I'm just scrolling back through my emails. There was definitely something about Mum. Ah – here it is. "Somewhat reliant on alcohol, though nothing diagnosed, and the possibility that she may have used drugs as a crutch at some point." Again, no concrete evidence, just suspicions and reports from a neighbour. And that's all there is, I'm afraid. But, as I say, you can rest assured about this,' she said again. 'Twenty-eight days, then it's no longer your problem.'

Rest assured. Very easy to say, but not so easy in practice. As we turned out of the parking lot and re-set the sat nav for the hospital, we were both silently contemplating possibilities for the next twenty minutes of what looked like being a twenty-five-minute journey. I'd no idea what was going through Mike's mind (same as what was going through mine no doubt – *here we go again*) but I was also once again questioning the validity of these types of placement. They gave no security to a child – not if there was no certainty that they would be going home at the end of it – but almost of equal importance was that it made normal life extremely difficult for a foster carer.

Respite and emergency placements aside, of course, when Mike and I took on a new child, during the early days and weeks we spent the time learning slowly about their personality and needs. We started with the basics. A list of rules, a mutually agreed list of expectations (bed making, teeth cleaning, language, etc.) and tackled all the smaller problems first (not least any recalcitrance when it came to rules and expectations). This set up a routine, a pattern and a rhythm to daily life that allowed the major things to reveal themselves over time and our subsequent goals for helping a child take back control of themselves. By then, hopefully, we had built up a sufficiently close relationship with the child that would better help us understand what made them tick and support them to work through their problems. This was key, because it was a system that gave us the opportunity to be 'parents' above all else. To create a nurturing environment, enabling the child to start to relax a little, and, crucially, hopefully, to place some trust in us. They would hopefully by then see that we were a safe place to be and that's when the real work would begin.

A twenty-eight-day placement made almost all of this impossible. The carers were expected to do only very prescribed types of work with the child and it was made clear to the child from the outset that they were not making a home with you. Yes, you were expected to teach them about family dynamics, and house rules, and how they could best manage their behaviour so that they could operate effectively within their own home, but this was part of a package that was rather hands-off for the foster family and included visits by various professionals, on a twice-weekly or even daily basis, to do similar and/or complementary work with them. But whatever the actual work involved, the problem (at least to my mind) was the same – it was a structure that didn't allow time to build trust, to nurture, or to explore the root of a child's problems. To be perfectly honest, I hated it. It made me feel more like a B&B owner than a carer.

As the now more familiar scenery rolled on by again, I shared my thoughts with Mike. 'Oh *gawd*,' I said. 'I'm wobbling a bit now. Have we just made a mistake?'

He grinned. 'You are a case, Case,' he told me. 'All this thinking! This is a job we've agreed to do. And do in the way we're *supposed* to do. Can't you, just for once, just accept this as a piece of work with a child that's going to last twenty-eight days? You know, we've only ourselves to blame if we make it more than it is.'

'You mean more in time? No way, Mike! I'm firm about that.'

'No, I don't mean in time – I mean in emotional investment. I mean more in the sense that, when it comes to day twenty-eight, you've become so emotionally involved that if things *don't* work out with the girl's mum, you get so weighed down with guilt and your usual "only I can see this through" mania that you can't give her up, and I have to speak very, very sternly to you.'

'That's a long speech.'

'Remember it. We can't be everything, to every child, every time. Best we keep in mind that we're just a step on the journey.'

'Your destination is ahead,' said the sat nav.

Chapter 2

We arrived at the hospital just as the rush hour was starting, but you'd never have known it in this semi-rural, out-of-the-way place. At first glance, you'd never know it was a hospital, either. It looked more like a manor house, with an equally grand garden: all mature trees, dappled shade and designer flower beds.

I only knew differently because I'd been here before. Our second ever foster child, Sophia (who had a multitude of problems that we felt at a loss to help with), had come here when she'd left us and I remembered driving up to the entrance as if it had been yesterday, as it had been such an emotionally charged day. It also occurred to me that we were here to collect another equally troubled soul – same gender, similar age – but making the journey in the other direction. Were we right to take this girl on, or had we acted too hastily?

Head over heart, I reminded myself as we approached the entrance, just as I'd told Ty a few minutes earlier.

Our long-term foster child Tyler had just had his eighteenth birthday. The time when, legally, if he was no longer in education, he would be expected to fly the nest. The very idea seemed unimaginable to all of us. Ty, who had come to us aged eleven, after being arrested for stabbing his stepmother, was our 'foster' son only in name. I don't know why, among all the kids who we'd opened our homes and hearts to, but it was obvious early on that we would never let him go. In reality he was as much 'one of ours' now as our own kids.

As such, and as he was the only one of them at home now, I'd called him to fill him in straight away; this was an unusual set-up for us all, after all, and it was important that he was fully on-message.

'It's difficult to explain the twenty-eight-day thing,' I'd told him, 'but it's very much a temporary set-up. So the idea is to just work with this girl on that basis, as caretakers – so it's not about trying to form the usual bonds with her. Like I said, it's difficult, but I'll try to explain more tomorrow. For now, just be polite and welcoming when we get back with her.'

He'd laughed. 'As opposed to what, Mum?' he wanted to know. 'Anyway, I won't be here. I'm just about to head over to Denver's. But, yeah, it's all cool.'

Cool. That was the thing. To keep cool and detached. But as soon as we stepped inside the building I knew my heart would try its level best to rule my head. Not good.

The reception of the hospital was exactly as I remembered it. Tastefully decorated, subdued lighting, smart blue cubic seating. And at its centre, seated next to a uniformed nurse, a kind of sun: a beautiful smiling child who seemed to light the whole place up. Not the cowed, nervous wreck of a girl I'd half expected. No, in her place was a girl with a head of bouncing, blonde-coloured curls, who looked straight at me, from a pair of the palest blue eyes I'd ever seen, and then stood, without prompting, to greet us. She was around my height. Possibly an inch taller. Which I'm obviously used to but in this case only enhanced the impression that there was a maturity about this thirteen-year-old girl.

'You must be Mr and Mrs Watson,' she said. 'Thank you so much for agreeing to have me. I'm so grateful.'

I was taken aback even more, and not just by how articulate she was. She sounded so self-assured that I almost dropped into a curtsey.

'Lovely to meet you, Harley,' I said, recovering myself. 'And please, call me Casey. And this is Mike,' I added, turning to him. 'No need for thanks, sweetheart, I'm just pleased we're able to help.'

The nurse had stood up as well and now produced a large holdall from beside the seat. 'All Harley's things are here,' she said. 'Don't forget your laptop is in the side pocket and sit on it,' she added to Harley with a grin. Then, returning to us, 'It's been a pleasure looking after her. There are just some notes for you to take with you at the desk, but then that's about it, I think. You all ready to go then, Harley?'

The girl smiled sweetly and, again, full of composure, she held out her hand to shake towards the nurse. 'I'm all set,' she said. 'Thank you so much for all you've done, and please tell Doctor Dave I said goodbye.'

'Oh, come *here*,' the nurse said, pulling Harley in for a hug. 'Doctor Dave will miss you just as much as I will, but we definitely *don't* want to see you back here. And I mean that in the nicest possible way, okay?'

It seemed she wasn't alone. By the time we'd signed our lives away and collected the paperwork, there had been further heartfelt goodbyes, as more people – staff and fellow patients by the look of it – seemed to appear specifically with the intention to wish Harley well. She'd obviously already touched a few hearts here. Though I noticed a certain stiffness about her too. As if she was not entirely comfortable at being touched.

I noted that, and also that she was silent once we climbed into the car and set off again, immediately plugging herself, via a pair of earbuds, into a mobile phone. She obviously wasn't up for mundane chit-chat with strangers either and I couldn't blame her. It had been a very emotional time for her, clearly.

I was also thankful for our sakes. Better she be plugged into whatever she was listening to than us all have to endure the sort of award conversation that would have been fine for a short trip, but not so great on a long journey – especially given why we all knew she was coming home with us. A very big elephant to have travelling in the car with us.

No, I thought. Better to get her home, settle her in and take things as they came. In the meantime we could relax and all draw breath for a while.

It was to turn out to be a very short while indeed.

Mike had only been driving for ten minutes or so, but, despite the coffee, I could already feel myself dozing off. (It had been a long emotional day, after all.) Which was why, when Mike yelled 'What the *hell*?', it genuinely made me jump, and I turned my head, following the direction of his horrified gaze through the rear-view mirror, to see Harley, no longer plugged into her earbuds, but jumping – literally *leaping* – from the moving car.

It all happened so fast that I could still see the image on my retina – a single fluid movement of the door opening and Harley lunging, then tumbling, out. I'd never even heard the seat belt click open.

'Oh my God!' I cried. 'Mike!'

'What the *hell*?' he said again. He slammed the brakes on, pressed the hazards and pulled the car over to the kerb, while I watched Harley bounce down the road, like a rag doll, behind us.

He unbuckled his seat belt, as did I. 'I can't believe that just happened,' he said, as we both scrambled out of the car. 'Jesus! Thank God I was slowing down for the junction!'

'Thank God no one was coming the other way!' I added, as we jogged back up the road to where Harley had come to rest. 'Should we phone for an ambulance, you think?'

'Let's check her out first,' Mike said, kneeling down as he got to her. She was trying to sit up, but looked stunned and confused. Had she done it in some sort of unconscious fugue? We were as lost for words as we had ever been in our fostering careers. And more than a little shaken up ourselves.

'Lay still for a minute, love,' Mike said, placing an arm on her upper back to support her.

She shrugged his hand off with a sharp twist of her back. I noted that too. 'No, it's fine. I'm okay,' she answered. Though she clearly wasn't; the whole right side of her face was badly grazed; smeared with dirt and bits of grit, and already weeping blood.

'You're far from okay, love,' I said. 'It's just a good job there were no other cars behind us.' And even as I said that, another vehicle had to swerve and slam on their brakes to avoid us all huddled in the middle of the road. The driver slowed and wound down his window.

'You all okay?' he asked anxiously. 'Do you need me to phone for an ambulance?'

'I'm *fine*,' Harley said again, scrabbling onto all fours, then to her feet. With that, and our first aid training, it seemed fairly obvious that there'd be no need to take her to A&E.

'It's okay,' Mike said just as I was about to. 'Nothing appears broken and we've just left a hospital. I think we'll get her back there to get checked out, but thank you.'

Let Me Go

'I'm *fine*,' Harley said a third time as the man drove off. 'Why can't anyone just let me go ahead and kill myself? *God*!'

Something heavy settled in the pit of my stomach. A profound sense of foreboding, I imagined, which felt like a stone. I proffered a hand in case she felt unsteady on her feet, but she batted that away too. I could see that her leggings were torn and one side of her hoodie had been streaked with black, oily marks from the road surface. *Go ahead and kill myself*. Great.

But I knew better than to tell someone with mental health issues not to be silly, let alone a child we had only just met, so instead I focused on the mundane.

'Oh dear, look at your lovely hoodie,' I said, standing back to give her space. 'I imagine that will need a couple of washes. And your face is all scratched. Ouch, it looks pretty painful! Or, at least it will be. Let's get you into the car again and we'll go back to see the nurses; see what they can do.'

Harley limped back to the car and clambered in, wincing. If nothing else, she'd be stiff and bruised tomorrow. And I'd wake up wondering if what had just happened could have possibly just happened. And what if there *had* been a car coming the other way? What had we just done in taking on this kid? 'Yeah, they'll most likely keep me there,' she said as she clicked on her seat belt. I thought so too. They clearly couldn't tell us she was fine, could they? She'd just tried to kill herself again!

'So at least I won't be a burden to you after all,' she added, smiling sweetly.

I noticed Mike flick the tiny child-lock switch as she did so, then head round to do the other side too. But I decided I should go for belt and braces. 'A burden? You absolutely are *not* a burden, sweetie, but it is best we get you checked out, and I'm sure you'll understand why I'm going to get in the back with you this time. I can't believe you did that, honestly.'

I climbed in and she looked across at me as if I were a bit dim. 'Why can't you believe that?' she asked. 'Didn't they tell you I want to die?'

I didn't want to answer that, but this was definitely not a time for small talk, so once I'd found a pack of tissues and suggested that she use them – fresh beads of bright red blood were still forming and trickling down her face – I was relieved when she picked up the phone and earbuds she'd abandoned to do her death-defying leap; it at least allowed me to sit and try and process what she'd just done. Not to mention think again just how wrong they clearly were about her mental state.

Ten minutes later, however, we were in for another shock. While Harley was whisked away to have the wound on her face cleaned and dressed, Mike and I, having explained to the receptionist what had happened, were asked to sit and wait. Five minutes later, we were shown into the manager's office, which was occupied by a woman who introduced herself as Mrs Raine.

'I'm the manager,' she elaborated. 'I've just come off the phone to Doctor Phelps. And you'll be pleased to hear that, after assessing the situation, we've decided that we won't be bringing Harley back as an inpatient. The discharge stands, and if the nurses uncover anything from the accident that needs further treatment, we'll be suggesting you go to your local accident and emergency department.'

I was stunned. *Pleased to hear?* 'But it *wasn't* an accident,' I pointed out, a little more shrilly than I intended. 'We've already explained what happened and I imagine she has too. Harley opened the door of a moving vehicle and jumped out *on purpose.* So I really don't understand why she isn't getting readmitted. She clearly isn't well yet. In fact,' I continued, 'she actually said that she was *determined* to kill herself. She must have duped everyone here into thinking she was safe and able to leave.'

Mrs Raine smiled at us both, albeit grimly. 'Mrs Watson,' she said, 'Harley has never stopped threatening to kill herself. She says it daily. But the fact is that she has been through all the tests, had all the counselling, been seen by a full team of psychiatrists and psychologists, and she doesn't have a diagnosable mental health problem. Her problems are environmental and care-seeking.'

Care-seeking, that old chestnut. I bristled at the term. Actually that *new* old chestnut, because it was a phrase I'd first encountered only recently, at a new course I'd been on; the new politically correct term for what we'd

23

always known as 'attention-seeking', because, they explained to us, that term was now derogatory because it indicated that a child would do anything, good or bad, just to get recognition – to get attention. Giving it a new name, of course, also gave it a new PC explanation. Which we duly had explained to us. In the new landscape of care there was a shift in the use of language and in this case it was all about positivity. No behaviour a child displayed could be seen, henceforth, as negative, because no matter what a child did, it wasn't to get attention – it was only because they 'needed love and care'.

I wasn't convinced at the meeting and I wasn't convinced now. Yes, it was obviously a good thing to approach a child with positivity, but there was potentially a dangerous side to it too. Prolific self-harmers were practically given a green light to do what they did and nobody would be officially allowed to get angry or upset about it, because it was simply 'care-seeking' behaviour.

I had railed to Mike about it at the time, and at some length, the bottom line being that if a child is hurting themselves, I believe 'angry' and 'upset' are two emotions that anyone can justifiably feel. So, positive, right now, I was definitely not. In fact, I was very close to asking Mrs Raine how she managed to conclude that Harley didn't have a mental health problem when within half an hour of us taking her she'd jumped, fully intentionally, out of a moving vehicle. Surely, common sense told her – as it was definitely telling me – that the fact that she did so meant she *did* have a mental health problem, at least as most normal people would describe it? It didn't matter a jot, actually, whether they prefixed it with 'attention' or 'care' – she was either seeking help because she needed it, or she was genuinely trying to die. Either way, that surely meant the right 'environment' for her was *here*, where she was contained for her own safety.

I didn't trust myself to speak without ranting, however, so was glad when Mike stepped in instead.

'Environmental, care-seeking or otherwise,' he said firmly, 'this girl just threw herself out of our car on a busy road. It's only pure luck that she wasn't seriously injured, or worse. Surely she must need some form of continuing professional help? And in a secure environment, for that matter, too.'

'Ah, but was it pure luck?' Mrs Raine asked, seeming to warm to her subject. 'In our experience, Harley can be very manipulative and she's very clever. It's not the first time she's done something extremely dramatic and luckily – there but for the grace of God, etc., etc. – she hasn't been seriously injured. You will have noticed that she jumped out only when the car was moving slowly. If she'd been serious about wanting to kill herself or sustain very serious injuries, she would have timed it so it happened at speed, wouldn't she? Perhaps on the motorway. Perhaps waiting till she saw a vehicle approaching from the other direction.'

We were both open-mouthed, wondering how to answer that, as she ploughed on. 'The thing is, Mrs and

Mrs Watson,' – at this point she leaned forward – 'our beds are in high demand for some very sick children. Children who've been diagnosed with severe mental health issues which we *can* treat, and I'm sorry, obviously, because I wish her only well, but I'm afraid Harley doesn't fit the criteria.'

So much for all those hugs and fond farewells, I thought miserably. 'But she's clearly sick,' I began, but Mrs Raine shook her head. 'We've done all we can do in the six weeks she's been here and to stay here any longer won't be good for her. We have no diagnosis, which means it's very hard to help her, and the truth is that she is – *was* – at risk of becoming institutionalised, adopting behaviours that she was picking up from other patients, none of which is going to help her in the longer term. I'm sorry, but this isn't the place for her.'

Yet we *were*? Frustrated as I was, I understood the point she was making. Without a professional diagnosis, there could be no treatment plan. And though help was clearly needed, *were* they best placed to provide it? Any hint that they weren't and it was really pretty obvious that their beds, which were precious, should be freed up for someone else who they felt more positive about treating. Passing on the problem, yes, but perhaps giving another child a better chance. And *this* child to a foster family. Us. Who must apparently take children leaping out of moving vehicles in their stride.

It seemed insane on the face of it, but resources were scarce. Short of refusing to take Harley – walking out, right then and there – we were all out of options bar accepting the problem and duly taking her home with us.

So, another ten minutes later, that was exactly what we had no choice but to do.

There was no trace now of her bright, polite greeting of an hour back (an hour and a lifetime back, it felt like) and though I opted to sit in the back again with her, Harley put her earbuds back in and said precisely nothing in response to my conversational gambits bar the odd 'right' or 'okay'. Mike tried too – as keen as I was to punch a hole in the oppressive silence.

'So, Harley? Let me guess,' he tried, as the motorway flashed past and I gave thanks for child locks, 'one of your parents was like me, perhaps? A Harley-Davidson fan?'

Mike loved absolutely everything about the iconic motorbike. Even if he didn't have the actual bike – for him to ever own one would be a divorcing matter, frankly – he was still a long-term devotee. He had the T-shirts and branded coffee mug to prove it.

The response from Harley, this time, was immediate. And unimpressed. 'Well, *duh*,' came the reply, followed by a slow, sarcastic hand clap. And that was it. No follow-up, no explanation, no further wish to engage.

We gave up then and the rest of the journey was made in silence. I couldn't even communicate to Mike via gestures, as I was on the wrong side for him to even make eye contact in the mirror. So it was that I was left to my own, troubled, thoughts.

I started to wonder about the family that this child had come from. I recalled Christine saying that the mother was widowed. So perhaps it *was* the dad, then, that had been the Harley-Davidson fan. Perhaps he'd even died in a tragic road accident? But there was nothing to be gained by weaving stories out of nothing. I'd find out the real story soon enough, I imagined. More important right now was to think about what we'd taken on and how we'd get through the next month. Not to mention the quiet night in we'd imagined. It already seemed like forever ago that little Annie and Oscar had gone. And here we were, plunged straight back into the deep end. Which was the nature of the job, so nothing out of the ordinary. But with a deep end that already felt substantially deeper and darker than it had a mere hour or so ago.

To pass the time as much as anything, I decided to text Tyler. Forewarned, after all, usually meant forearmed, and, in the circumstances, that seemed to make sense.

Hi, sweetie, I texted, *just to give you a heads-up, this girl looks like being more complicated than we thought. Just to warn you, she jumped from the car a while ago and is a bit bruised up. The plan is the same – she stays with us for twenty-eight days – but please try to ignore how she looks when we get home. I'll explain fully later on. xxx*

My phone beeped back within seconds.

OMG! Okay, Mum. I'll stick around at Denver's then, okay? Makes sense, right?

Which it did, though it saddened me and once again, I wondered if we'd just made a massive mistake, especially with the new baby coming too. I glanced across at Harley's battered, bruised and now swollen face and couldn't escape the feeling that we had. But it was too late for that now, I told myself sternly, and at least it was finite. That twenty-eighth day would come round soon enough, however dark the journey might be to get there.

Chapter 3

I tried to brighten my mood as we finally walked through the front door. We'd taken Harley on, and now we were home, it was a case of rolling up our sleeves and getting on with it. It seemed quiet though, without Tyler there, and specially in contrast to having the two little ones running around. Quiet and gloomy now the sky was growing dark as well.

'Right then,' I said brightly, as Harley followed into the hallway. 'Mike, why don't you head up with Harley's holdall?' I turned to her then and smiled. 'While I give you a quick downstairs tour so you can get your bearings first, yes? Then I'll help you sort your things out.'

She shook her head. 'If it's okay, I really just want to go to sleep. If you don't mind, that is,' she added, already turning and following Mike up. 'And I'll sort my things out in the morning. I'm really tired.'

'Oh, of course,' I agreed. 'You're bound to be tired. In fact, that might even be better actually, because your room's been in use – two little ones who only left us earlier today. So there's a fair bit of sorting out to be done in there – toys all over the place, and the put-you-up bed still up, and clothes and bits and bobs still in all the drawers. I'll just come up and quickly change your bed for you at least, if that's okay.'

Harley turned around and nodded, but I could see irritation on her face. Presumably at the thought of having to spend yet more time with us – me rambling on about her room (I was already aware that I was) and fussing about sorting beds out when she really did just want to be alone. We got up to the landing and Mike dropped the bag in the doorway. 'I'll leave you girls to it, then,' he said. 'Put the kettle on. Give me a shout if you need anything moving or whatever.'

By now I could have killed for a restorative mug of coffee, so I wasted no time in grabbing a clean duvet set from the airing cupboard; one more suited than what was on there for our unexpected guest. 'Butterflies!' I announced, 'much better than Peppa Pig and George and his dinosaur.'

Again, I got a nod and a flicker of a forced smile and then, unexpectedly, 'Little ones? As in tiny children? Did their mum not want them either, then? That's awful.'

It was the first bit of normal conversation I'd heard from Harley yet. She looked genuinely engaged, too, all of a sudden, looking down at the beds.

My turn to shake my head now. 'Not in this case, I'm glad to say. Not in most cases, actually – it's rare that a mum doesn't want a child, more often than not it's that they can't cope, for one reason or other,' I added, mindful of her own mother. 'But, no, in this case, we were just looking after the little ones while their parents were in hospital. They'd been hurt in a fire, and didn't have family close by to take care of them, so we said we'd look after them till they were well enough to come home.'

Harley nodded and said, 'Oh, I see', then went to look out of the bedroom window, where she remained while I stripped and re-made the bed, her question about the former residents clearly all she had to say. I didn't press her. She was obviously tired – both physically and mentally.

'There,' I said eventually, 'all done and ready. I'll sort the trundle bed out in the morning. Get it out of your way. But for now I'll say goodnight and let you get some sleep.'

'Thank you, I really am so tired,' she said and I could tell that she meant it. 'It was horrible trying to sleep in that hospital,' she added with a shudder. 'What with all the screaming and howling every night.'

I tried to imagine it. Screaming and howling in 'asylums' was the stock in trade of movies. But what was life on a long-term mental health ward really like? Just like that, I imagined, at least some of the time, anyway. It wasn't as if they could soundproof every wall. It might have looked serene to us, or any other passing visitor, but we'd only seen the grounds and reception area, hadn't we? Perhaps she was better off out of that place after all. But if she'd been keen to leave, then why risk being returned to them? It made no sense.

'Of course, sweetie,' I said. 'We'll sort everything out tomorrow. And in the meantime you get your head down and get some rest. What about something to eat though? Are you hungry at all? Or shall I bring you up a drink?'

'No, thank you,' she said politely. 'I'm not eating at the moment. And I'd just like to be on my own now.'

And with that, and a glance towards the door, I was dismissed. I just hoped she wasn't going to do anything like jump out of the window. Instinct told me, however, that today's bolt was shot; and perhaps Mrs Raine was right about Harley only 'trying' to kill herself, in any case. I had to hope so. Short of locking her in a padded cell, there was little else I could do. And what did she mean about 'not eating at the moment'? Did she mean as in now? Or today? Or for the foreseeable future? Had she put herself on hunger strike? So many unanswered questions. What a situation to suddenly find ourselves in.

Which was why, coffee on board, and Mike in front of the telly, I wasted no time in calling Christine Bolton. She had already texted on our way home to tell me to call her when I could. *Even if it's late*, she'd added. *I'll leave my mobile switched on*.

I guess she thought it was the least she could do. Though I knew she'd be unprepared for what I told her.

'Oh my God, Casey!' was her first reaction, echoing Tyler's earlier. 'I just can't believe it! I genuinely do not know what to say to you.'

'Well, you couldn't have known,' I said. 'Any more than we could. I mean, it's not something you really prepare for, is it? A kid leaping from the back of a moving car. So, there's nothing you or anyone could have done about it.'

There were a few moments of what I assumed was a guilty silence. 'But if I'd known the girl was still like this, I would have absolutely point-blank refused to take responsibility for her. I feel I've been sold down the swanny, frankly. God, I'm *so* sorry, Casey. Looks like this Harley has fooled us all – the professionals, too.'

'Not according to the manager,' I told her. 'She talked about Harley's threats to kill herself – and attempts to – as if it were all just, I don't know, business as usual. And according to the psychologist, there isn't anything diagnosable wrong with her. It's all just "environmental", whatever that means.'

Christine huffed just as I had. 'I presume what it means is that they've washed their hands of her.'

'Quite. But the fact remains, ill or not, this girl clearly intends to harm herself and I don't know how we manage that. It certainly doesn't seem the ideal starting point for trying to work with her to be able to get back home to her mother, does it?'

'No, it doesn't,' Christine said, but then, more firmly, 'Look, we were told that there was no longer any significant risk with Harley. That's obviously wrong – she's already proved that – but all you and Mike can do is your job. Do the obvious, like locking away medicines,

34

keeping an eye on your knives, razors, etc., but if she leaves the house, you can't forcibly stop her, as you know. Just do as you would with any other child, okay? Always give her a coming-home time and if she isn't back by then, phone the emergency duty team and the police, and report her as missing and vulnerable. She has a mobile, I'm assuming?'

'Oh yes. And it's her best friend by the looks of it. So no worries there.'

'Good. Make sure she gives you the number as soon as possible.'

'Oh, you can be sure I shall be doing that.' I grimaced at the thought of what we might have to deal with, but at the same time I knew it was absolutely my job. 'And what if she leaves the house having first told us she intends to do herself harm?' I asked.

'Same answer,' Christine said. 'You must let her leave if she insists. Remember that case a few years ago when a foster carer dragged a child back from an upstairs window they intended to jump from?'

I did. The child reported it and the foster carers, ridiculously, in my book, had to fight an assault charge. 'I do indeed,' I said. 'But I understand, I get it. Follow protocol with the police, EDT (the Emergency Duty Team) and my own reporting procedures to you, and then just keep my fingers and toes crossed that nothing awful happens.'

'Exactly. As will I,' she said. 'Anyway, I'd better leave you to it. I'm not sure of her name, but I imagine you'll hear from Harley's social worker sometime tomorrow. Let's ride this out and see what we can do to help, yes? And in the meantime, please just try to see this for what it is, Casey. And remember, you and Mike can only do what you can do. Keep that uppermost in your minds at all times.'

Christine was right. I had no choice in the matter, did I? We'd do our best to keep her safe – at least make things as safe as we could for her – and once I was off the phone to Christine, Mike and I discussed how we'd do that.

'Like we said before though, Case,' Mike pointed out, 'this is very short-term, and at the end of it we have Kieron and Lauren and the baby to think about, so let's just get together with the social worker, knock up a risk assessment, or whatever it is they call them these days, and get on with it.'

I laughed at that. Mike wasn't one for paperwork, at least not my kind of paperwork. He was a whizz at stock-taking and numbers, but the pen and paper stayed at work as far as he was concerned. I glanced up towards the bedroom above us and sighed. 'For all the hiding of knives, sharps, and pills, the way things are going the poor thing might die of bloody starvation or dehydration if she doesn't accept any food or drink,' I said. 'If she wasn't hungry, she would surely have just said she wasn't hungry. Not eating "at the moment" sounds more like she's deliberately starving herself. Or she feels she doesn't need to because she knows she's not long for this world. *Seriously*, Mike,' I added. 'This isn't funny!'

For he was smiling. 'Oh, love, you're so dramatic!' he said. 'It's been what? Three hours or so since we met her? I hardly think she'll be wasting away already. If you're that worried, go take her something up. Leave it outside her door for her.'

I did exactly that. A glass of fruit squash and a plateful of snacks. I then knocked. 'Harley, love,' I whispered, 'I know you weren't hungry, but I've left you a few bits out here for you to take in, in case you get peckish or thirsty through the night.'

There was no reply so I knocked again. 'Harley, did you hear me, love?'

'Thank you,' she said finally, 'I'll get them in a minute.'

And when I checked, an hour later, she'd duly taken them in. Which at least gave me some cause for relief. Perhaps I was being overly dramatic. Perhaps the psychologist was right. Perhaps she had absolutely no intention of killing herself. Perhaps it was all about being separated from her mother – 'care-seeking' as they put it – and perhaps, after the rejection of being forcibly discharged, her leap from the car was just her way of letting *us* know that she *still* needed care, that she needed our help. Like putting down a marker. Or a line in the sand. If so, I thought gamely, bring it on.

Chapter 4

'Mum, where's the pickle gone?'

It was late morning on Wednesday – day three of Harley's placement – and while I was busy knocking up a cheese sandwich for her, Tyler was speed-assembling a packed lunch for himself. 'Seriously,' he added, shunting bottles and jars around the bottom of the fridge. 'I *need* it. I have to be out the door by twelve or I'm going to be late!'

'You *need* it?' I asked, grinning at him. 'Why don't you just grab some ketchup instead? Time was when a glug of that would have been fine with anything. We don't *have* any pickle, love. Dad finished up the last of it and I haven't been able to do my shop yet, have I?' Something I was hoping to be able to do later on – at least if Mike managed to get away from work on time, like he'd promised.

Tyler sighed dramatically as he pulled out some mustard. 'Hello – there are *computers*? And time was,

Mummy dear, when you'd have made my packed lunch *for* me.' He sighed again. 'Where, oh where, have those golden days gone?'

I laughed as I grabbed another couple of slices of bread and began buttering them for him. 'Those days, my darling boy, have suffered the same fate as the jar of pickle. They no longer exist, they have ceased to be.'

Tyler grinned and nodded towards the pile of cheese I'd grated. 'So I noticed,' he said. 'My loving mother has now been replaced by a chambermaid, slash waitress, slash carer – of an invisible child. Have you Harry Pottered her into a cupboard under the stairs or something? Seriously, I'm beginning to wonder if she even exists.'

He had a point. Over the last sixty-odd hours, I'd taken food upstairs at least half a dozen times, depositing it outside Harley's bedroom door every time as if an offering for a vengeful god. Yet of Harley herself, I had seen very little. She had twice opened the door enough for me to see her, if little more, and such visits as she'd made to the bathroom had been mostly conducted when no one else was around. It really was as if she was treating our home like she were in some fancy hotel, a feeling that – worryingly – I was struggling to shake off, because middle-aged women moaning about kids treating their homes 'like hotels' was a look I really didn't want to be accused of liking. I kept having to remind myself that she was a vulnerable, suicidal teen and not simply a 'problem' that had been 'dumped' on us.

Tyler, who had yet to clap eyes on her, obviously, clearly had no such internal wrangles.

'Well, what else am I meant to do, Ty?' I asked, frustrated with myself. 'I need to make sure she eats, even if she does refuse to leave her room.'

Tyler shrugged as he wrapped his lunch in a square of foil. 'I dunno, Mum, but you aren't really making sure she eats, are you? You're making sure you provide food, but how do you know she's eating it? She could be flinging it out of the window into next door's garden, for all you know. Anyway, I'm out of here. Don't forget the pickle!'

I was still staring at the tray full of food after Tyler had kissed my cheek and left. He was right. I had no idea if Harley had eaten any of the stuff I'd left for her. I had simply relied on the information available to me: the empty plates being put back outside her bedroom door. In fact, I'd only seen her once outside her room since she'd come to us, scurrying across the landing to the bathroom, in satin pyjamas, at 5 a.m. this morning, with her mobile phone clutched in her hand. Not entirely out of the ordinary – teenagers never seemed to go anywhere without their phones these days, the loo included – but it was clear this situation needed nipping in the bud; it would be impossible to help her if I never actually interacted with her, and two days seemed more than enough for her to re-orient herself and engage with us. Tyler was right: I needed to get in there and start making some ground rules.

'Harley!' I called, as I knocked at her door, the tray balanced carefully on my free hand. 'I'm sorry, sweetie, I know you're still feeling a bit rubbish, but I have to come in, love, okay?'

'Hang on!' I heard back, followed by a scramble and then the door opening. 'What is it?' she asked, her face squeezing through around four inches of opening.

I smiled at the absurdity. It was as if I were a pestering cold caller, turning up on her doorstep unannounced to try and sell her something, and who she was absolutely not going to let in. Well, I wasn't a cold caller. This was my house, I had been asked to take care of her, and she wasn't going to stop me, ill or not.

'I don't want to push my way in, sweetheart, but I do need to come in,' I told her. 'Only for a moment or two. I need to just have a quick look at your scratches and to make sure everything is alright in here. And get your mobile phone number.'

Those cold blue eyes looked at me with new suspicion. 'Why do you need to have my number? That's private.'

'I'm not suggesting I invade your privacy, love,' I said nicely. 'But we need to exchange mobile numbers because that's one of the rules.'

'Why?'

'So if you go out we can keep in touch with one another. I'm not asking for your phone, or even to see it, just your number so I can text you if you're out and I need to. It's not the Spanish Inquisition. Just part of my job, I'm afraid, so can you open the door, please? Then we can get it over with.'

Harley scowled, then pulled the door open and turned away from me in one single movement, marching across to the bed and standing in front of it, arms folded across her chest. 'Oh my God,' she said dramatically, 'it's as bad as being back at the hospital, this is. Why can't I simply be left alone?'

I placed the tray on the bedside table as my eyes scanned the room. 'You know why,' I said as I made a point of checking out the side of her face. 'Did you clean your grazes and put more of the antiseptic cream on?'

'Yes, of course I did,' she said petulantly. 'And why? *Why* can't you leave me alone? What difference does it make? Do you seriously think you can stop me from killing myself if I wanted to?'

She was disarmingly articulate – a very different prospect from most of the children we took care of. And also poised, very beautiful and seemingly in control – all very much at odds with the question she'd just asked me, which made it difficult to know how best to respond to it.

'No, love, I don't suppose I could,' I plumped for finally. 'I don't suppose anyone could, but I'm really hoping that you don't decide to do that. I can't pretend to know how you're feeling, but what I do know is that no matter how bad things seem, they can always get better.'

She rolled her eyes at this. 'You really don't understand, do you?' she answered, stepping across to the chest of drawers and calmly opening the top one. 'And here, before you search my room, here's the food you've been leaving me. I don't want to eat, because I don't want to live. So, since you're here, you might as well have it back.'

She started lobbing bits of fruit, packets of crisps and empty side plates onto the bed. Of the sandwiches I'd previously made her there was no sign, but, as if reading my mind, just as I began asking, 'Where's all the—' she nodded towards the window. 'It's important to feed the birds at this time of year,' she said archly.

It wasn't, actually, I thought. There were berries ripening absolutely everywhere. But blow me, Tyler had been right. 'I did drink the juice,' she continued, 'and I got water from the bathroom so don't worry, I'm not going to die on you *just* yet.'

She was mocking me, and the temptation to become irritable was immense, but I reminded myself that she was a deeply damaged soul and that deeply damaged youngsters often did their level best to inspire everyone around them to dislike them. I also looked at the food now laid out for my inspection and decided it could stay just where it was.

'I'm so sorry that you're feeling like this, I really am,' I told her. 'And I know you don't know me, but I'm here for you, okay? Here to talk. Here to listen. Here in any way you need me to be here for you, okay? Oh, and one other thing, love,' I added, as she thumped the drawer shut again. 'Your social worker is going to be here later on today. I'm sure you'll want to talk to her at least, won't you?'

'*Tessa*?' she said, eyes wide with disbelief. 'Why on earth would I want to talk to *her*?'

I had no answer to that. 'I don't know, Harley, do I? I know nothing about you. So tell me. Why *don't* you want to talk to her? I'm guessing from your reaction that you have a pretty good reason.'

'Because she doesn't *listen*,' she said. 'She just thinks I'm "playing games".' She lifted her arms and put the words into two-finger quote marks. 'Would *you* want to speak to someone who said that about you? And to your *face*? So, no, I don't want to speak to her, thank you.'

'Well, that's your choice, love,' I told her. 'I can't make you see her, but, you know, at some point you are going to have to come out and join the real world. Now,' I said, pulling my own phone from my pocket, 'can I take your number down, love?'

Harley shook her head, but this time it seemed to be in sadness rather than defiance. And I knew what she was thinking as she grumpily ran through all the digits – that I really didn't get it. That the real world was exactly what she was trying to escape.

And who was I to argue with her reasoning, either? I really didn't know the first thing about her, let alone the complexity of the situation that had brought her to my door. But at least I'd know more on the arrival of her social worker, who, according to the brief call she'd made to me yesterday, would be arriving, and hopefully filling me in a bit, at two, even if the girl in her charge didn't want to see her.

Tessa Halliday, in fact, arrived at more like twenty past, and as I watched her walk down the path, glasses bouncing off her chest from a glinting silver chain, instinct told me that the stressed-out expression on her face was not so much related to the fact that she was running late as a more or less permanent state – something I saw a lot more these days than I used to. She looked hot, too, three-quarter-length trousers clinging to her shins, and had the air of someone who regularly found herself thinking that she'd probably made the wrong career choice. Perhaps she had – the enormous neon-striped raffia tote bag on her shoulder looked as if it would be more at home on a Spanish beach. Perhaps it had been until only recently. Perhaps she carried it as a talisman, a reminder of happier times.

I opened the door before she got to it and beamed brightly at her – negative vibes could be horribly contagious. 'I'm Casey,' I chirruped. 'Come on in, kettle's on.'

'Thanks,' she puffed, as if she'd jogged rather than driven. 'So muggy today, isn't it? I'm roasting! So I'll just have a glass of water, if that's okay.'

'Water it is, then,' I said. And, gesturing, I added, 'Go on into the living room. Make yourself at home while I just go and fetch it. Though I've squash, if you'd prefer that? Or juice?'

'No, *really*,' she said. 'Just water will be fine,' and, rightly or wrongly, I got the impression that just being here was a pain for her, let alone being plied with exotic drink choices.

It was an impression that didn't change when I returned to the living room to find her manhandling a buff folder out of the incongruous beach bag with a scowl on her face – it kept snagging on various frayed bits and refusing to come out.

'So,' she said, as she finally liberated what I presumed was Harley's file, 'I gather Madam isn't gracing us with her presence?'

That 'Madam', I thought. It didn't sit well with me – sounded loaded. But I reminded myself that I was in no position to judge just what kind of load Tessa Halliday carried. I shook my head, reserved judgement. 'Not right now.'

She hooked up her glasses, took out some paperwork and placed it in front of her. 'Not that I thought she would, to be honest,' she said. 'She hates me, the world and all who reside in it, at the moment.'

'Sounds as if you know Harley quite well then,' I proffered.

Tessa nodded. 'Been about eighteen months since I got involved with the family,' she explained. 'Maybe a little longer. Harley had suffered at the hands of some quite nasty bullies. Both at school and online, this was. We got called in by the school one day after she'd refused to get changed for a sports lesson and it had come out that she'd been cutting herself. Seriously enough for them to report it to us – no doubt you'll see for yourself soon enough – and all over, everywhere. Arms, legs and torso. I'd bet there's not two inches of skin – of the skin she can get to – that hasn't been mutilated in some way.'

Something about the matter-of-fact way she described this disturbed me. It was as if she were relating a news report to me, not speaking about the fragile young girl who was lying in her room only six feet above our heads. I had seen the results of self-harm many times before but it was always shocking enough to ensure that I'd never become desensitised to it; no less sad seeing perfect young skin being so scarred. Sadly, it sounded as though Tessa had. I wondered what else she'd seen during her own years at the coalface.

'Right,' I said, 'well, as I said when we spoke, she changed into pyjamas when she got here – long sleeves and legs – so as yet I've seen nothing. In fact, I've seen very little of her at all. I know very little about her and what makes her tick, which is why I'm very keen to hear about her background. So, initially you were just work-ing with the family then? What did that look like? Anything you can tell me will be really helpful.'

'Well, as I said, the cutting was very serious – poten-tially life-threatening in some cases, so much so that her mother apparently had to call an ambulance quite a few times to get Harley rushed into hospital for urgent treat-ment. My remit was to try to work with them to get to the root cause and to help Harley find less invasive ways of dealing with her problems. However, things escalated when Millie left home. She—'

'I'm sorry, who?' I interrupted. 'Millie, you say?'

'Millie as in Harley's older sister. There are just the two of them. Six-year age gap but they were apparently very close. Since the death of their father – Harley would have been around three when that happened—'

'How did he die?'

'In a motorcycle accident. He was a biker apparently. All very sad and so on,' she added, not looking sad at all. 'And it seems Millie was very much the glue that held this fractured family together, because the mother was, and still is, I suspect, addicted to prescription drugs and alcohol – it seems she never really recovered from the shock of her husband's death – so it was Millie who dressed Harley each morning and took her to school, made sure she had something to take for her lunch and had a cooked meal when she got home. But, as would be expected, Millie fell in love and eventually moved out. You can't blame the girl,' she added, even though I wasn't about to. 'It was far too much responsibility for her at such a young age.'

I let out a big breath and leaned back in my seat. There was definitely a lot more going on here than just a child being bullied at school, bad enough though that was. 'So the serious cutting – the hospital treatment – this happened *after* Millie left?'

'Actually, no,' Tessa replied, 'she'd already been doing that, and it really upset her sister, obviously, but after she left, Harley upped her game. That's when she was first rescued from a bridge over a motorway. Personally,

I thought it was a ploy to get Millie to come home – the witness didn't think she was actually going to jump – but–' she spread her hands – 'I just don't know anymore. She seems dead set on harming herself – she's proven that over and over – but whether or not she actually intends to *kill* herself, I'm not so sure.'

'It seems the nurses and psychiatrists agree with you on that score,' I said, 'I think everybody assumes that Harley is attention-seeking, and yes, I *know* that's not PC to say these days, but that's the top and bottom of it. That's what it amounts to.'

Tessa's expression told me she thought I'd hit the nail on the head. 'Well, we can't argue with the professionals, can we?' she said. 'They must see thousands of kids presenting like Harley, so they'll know what they're looking at. Well, in theory. What can I say?'

Nothing I wanted to hear, that was for sure. In fact, the more I heard, the more despondent I felt. It was no wonder the mother felt at her wits' end. And as Tessa outlined the family situation in more detail it became clear that the perfect storm that had brought Harley to us had been brewing for some time. Her poor mother had suffered a terrible loss when her husband had died in that road accident and had consequently gone down a suffocating spiral of drink and drugs. Her eldest daughter, whom she relied on for everything, had now gone, and, crucially, it seemed, taking her boyfriend with her.

Because it seemed it wasn't just Millie who'd held the family together – her boyfriend Zar had apparently also been something of a rock for the family. In the last few months before he and Millie had left to set up home together, he'd even moved in with them, providing much-needed help with their always-behind rent, as well as contributing more than his fair share for all the bills and doing odd jobs around the house. 'I met him a couple of times,' Tessa told me. 'Lovely, lovely lad. He genuinely wanted to help support them, but, again, it was too big a job, not least because Mum didn't ever really acknowledge that she *needed* any help.' She tutted. 'Well, till she realised she *did*.'

'And I guess by then it was too late,' I said. I had a thought then. I knew Millie was still a teenager, so was her boyfriend as well? It seemed odd that he'd be in a position to help with the rent. 'Is Zar older than Millie?' I asked Tessa.

Tessa nodded. 'Mid-twenties. And mature, by all accounts. He certainly seemed that way to me. In fact, when they were first visited by social services, the on-duty social worker thought he was with the mother. Easy enough mistake to make, given how young Mum is – she's still only in her thirties now – and easy enough to see why Millie would be attracted to someone a bit older too – losing her dad that young meant she was probably looking for a father figure. But not a father – and it seemed pretty obvious to me that it was too much to expect the lad to take on a role like that.'

And perhaps understandably – because who could blame them, really? – the young couple had made the painful decision that enough was eventually enough and left to make a new life for themselves away from the burdens of the family.

'Does Millie stay in touch?' I asked, because it seemed so obvious to me that she would. She had clearly been the biggest influence on Harley's young life and for that to be ruptured so completely must have taken a huge toll. 'Maybe she's the one who is best placed to help Harley out of this. I know it's a lot of responsibility to place on such young shoulders, and making the decision to leave must have been a hard one, but—'

'That's just it,' Tessa said. 'Whether because of apathy or, more likely, self-preservation, Millie has now pretty much cut off all contact. They spoke often in the beginning, but it became less and less and I believe now that contact has pretty much stopped completely. I spoke to her myself just after she left and she was nothing if not forthright. Said she was sorry, but she just wasn't up to it anymore – that she needed some time out to have her own life, unencumbered by her mum and sister's problems.'

'Sounds a bit harsh,' I said, trying to imagine a scenario where someone would completely turn their back on their sibling. But even as I thought it, I knew the reality was that it did, sadly, happen. And in the world that I had made myself part of, the fostering world, it happened with depressing regularity.

But who was I to judge? I'd put money on the fact that if I asked her myself she'd tell me that the only way to get her mum to address her issues was, in her view, to *make* her face up to them – a dose of very necessary tough love. Plus, she'd clearly decided she'd done all she could, as had her boyfriend, and was bailing before she was sucked under herself.

Tessa nodded. 'I know. It does *sound* harsh,' she agreed, 'but all we can do now is work with what we've got, and respect the fact that Harley's sister and her partner have every right to make a life for themselves, and who knows – perhaps Millie is right, it will make Mum face up to and actually deal with her addictions. And though it's perhaps not ideal that Harley's no longer in a secure environment, given what's happened, I'm hoping the ticking clock will at least concentrate Mum's mind to really engage with the intensive work we are going to do with her, the plan being to hopefully get her to a point where she feels able to trust herself to look after Harley with minimal ongoing intervention.'

'But what if Harley is clinically depressed?' I asked. 'Can't they start her on some medication?'

'Tried that, a number of times, but she refuses to take it. The thing is, the general consensus, silly as it sounds, is that Harley actually thrives on the attention of the professionals. A kind of Munchausen's thing, if you like. She knows refusing meds will mean more time spent with doctors and refusing to speak to psychologists means more time spent with child and adolescent mental health services. Seems a ridiculous merry-go-round to anyone not on it, but for Harley, well, the proof seems to be in the pudding, doesn't it? Her "suicide" attempts are all just that. Attempts.'

I saw Tessa off soon after, feeling little had changed. She'd go away and continue her work with the mother, and, in the meantime, I would continue my 'caretaking' role – continuing to care for Harley's physical needs till the twenty-eight days (twenty-five days now, in fact) were up and she would 'hopefully' be returned home.

But for one thing, which could hardly escape anyone's notice – not all suicide attempts end in failure.

Chapter 5

Desperation shows itself in a variety of forms and it transpired that we were about to be introduced to some that even hardened carers like us had never encountered before.

At first, I was beginning to think that I could actually let my guard down. It was far from ideal for Harley to spend all her time shut away in her room, but at least I knew where she was, and that she was relatively safe. (I say 'relatively', because long experience has taught me that if a child wants to harm themselves they will find a way. If the idea takes root they can be astonishingly resourceful; a simple hair clip, a pen, even the edge of a drawer can cause significant damage for more well-practised self-harmers. However, other than take up camp beside Harley's bed, I certainly couldn't keep eyes on her 24/7.)

But taking on Harley wasn't just about keeping her safe. It was about trying to prepare her for a return to her mother. So it was on day four, the following morning, that I decided I wouldn't take no for an answer. I would somehow get into that room, plonk myself onto a chair and stay there for as long as I could.

Today, then, breakfast would be accompanied by a side order of Casey. Bearing a tray filled with yoghurt, cereal, berries and fruit juice, I went upstairs to her, knocked once, called out her name and walked in.

'Morning, sweetie!' I called as I set the tray down on the chest of drawers. 'Brought you some breakfast. And let me just open these curtains for you,' I added. 'It's a bit stuffy in here, isn't it? And it's absolutely *gorgeous* outside today. We seem to be having quite the Indian summer!'

I had no idea if Harley even knew what an 'Indian summer' was, but she was clearly unimpressed, grumbling to herself as she pulled herself up against her pillows. 'I'm not really hungry yet,' was all she said in response.

The 'yet' seemed promising. So she wasn't on hunger strike today, at least. 'No matter,' I trilled. 'Nothing on here that won't keep for a bit.' I sat on the dressing-table stool then and made a thing out of brushing imaginary bits from my leggings. 'You know, I was thinking you might like a bath or a shower this morning,' I went on. 'I can run you a nice bubbly bath if you'd like?'

Harley shrugged. 'I'm not fussed,' she said, looping her hair behind her ears and eyeing me suspiciously. 'I might get one a bit later or something. See how I feel.'

Better, I wanted to point out. You will feel *better* if you do. I didn't, though. 'Oh, well, that's absolutely fine,' I said instead. 'I'll just stay and chat for a bit, then. You know, it's been four days and I barely know anything about you! Time we caught up a bit, I think, don't you?'

Harley looked horrified. As if chatting to me would be the worst kind of torture. '*Okay*. I'll get a bath, then,' she said, her eyes darting around her messy room, 'and I'll clean this up. And I'll put my clothes away …'

Anything, clearly, to get me out of her room.

I smiled my brightest smile. 'That's good, sweetie. That would be great. I'd really appreciate it,' I added. 'But, *still* … Let's agree that we chat for at least ten minutes each day, shall we? Because you know, that's a very important part of my job and I wouldn't be doing it right if I didn't insist on it.'

This obviously struck a chord. 'I won't tell anyone if you don't, I promise,' she said in earnest. 'I'm just not one for chatting, but I promise I won't tell on you. If anyone asks, I'll tell them we chat all the time, every day.'

I didn't miss the irony of this exchange, even if she did. Here we were, chatting away – about her insistence on not chatting away. What a complicated child this was.

'Oh, I get that,' I reassured her. 'Not everybody is, are they? And it's not about being "told on", it's about me wanting to get to know you. So, let's see … how about I start … Hmm … Oh, I know. How about we chat about your sister? Millie, isn't it? How about you tell me about her? You must really miss her.'

I'd already figured that any mention of Millie's name would probably have an impact. It might cause a confrontation and, on the other hand, it might make her shut down. But any kind of response would, I decided, equal progress, even if only the proof that we were getting to some kind of nub regarding the effect of Harley's sister's disappearance. But neither happened. She stared at me, wide-eyed and open-mouthed, for a second, then her chin started to quiver and out came a torrent of tears.

'I told Tessa, and I'm telling you, *I don't want to talk about Millie*!' she said as she wept, 'She's dead to me,' she added, spitting the words out between sobs. '*Please. Please just leave me alone*!'

The poor girl was actually begging me to get out now, so I duly did. 'Okay,' I said from the doorway, 'we can leave it for now and I'm sorry if I upset you, sweetie. I'll see you in a bit, okay?'

Of course there was no answer. Any hope of further conversation had obviously now gone, as had the idea of getting a bath, I imagined, too. But even so, after I left her, I still felt I'd made a modicum of progress. Whatever I'd unleashed in mentioning Harley's sister's name to her was preferable to the sort of shutting down I'd seen so often in previous children – that kind of absence of emotion was altogether more chilling. No, if Millie's name could still provoke such an emotional reaction, then she was obviously still very much in Harley's thoughts. Which was something I could work with, though it didn't feel particularly edifying to still hear her anguished sobs from the bottom on the stairs. *Great job, Casey*, I told myself as I returned to the kitchen. Always a joy to make someone feel good first thing on a morning.

I sighed and picked up my cold, half-cup of coffee. Progress, yes, but it wasn't even nine in the morning and who knew how long it would be before we engaged again? And, in the meantime, I couldn't leave the house. Laundry, then. I'd tackle that instead.

As usual, I had my radio tuned into a golden era station in the conservatory, which was where my ironing pile and laundry baskets always hung out, and also as usual, I cranked up the volume so that I could sing along without assaulting anyone's ears.

It was a new radio; one with a retro cream leather casing, which Riley (my daughter) had treated me to the previous Christmas. A new-fangled one, too, that went by the name 'DAB', whatever that meant. Actually, I did know what 'DAB' meant, because my grandson Levi had told me. It was a dance move – more specifically, a 'hip-hop' dance move, where you dropped your head as far as you could into the crook of your shoulder, while raising both arms out to one side.

Somewhat confusing, then, that my new retro radio seemed to share the same name. I kept quiet about that particular observation, however, just in case asking the question made me look silly.

I spent a pleasant hour getting properly stuck in. Though I'd laundered the things the twins needed to take back home before they left us, I still had a backlog of bedding and towels, and some of my own collection of kiddie clothes they'd been wearing, and this was the perfect time to do so, it being such a perfect drying day. So, a second batch of dirty laundry in the washing machine, and dry clothes folded ready for ironing, I took the first basket of wet laundry out into the garden to hang on the washing line.

It really was gorgeous – the sort of late September day that comes without warning, just as you've accepted that summer's finally over – which in my case requires a great deal of acceptance. The sun was shining on the autumn canopy, leaves turning yellow, red and orange, and with the warm breeze Mother Nature had kindly provided also, I calculated that I could probably get all the bedding done within a few hours.

I was just stepping back inside when I heard the front door slam. Must be Tyler back, I thought, making a mental note to tell him off for slamming doors – before realising it might have done so because *this* door was open. *Though why back at this time?* was my second thought.

I walked into the hall, expecting to see him, and hear about some forgotten thing or other, but, as far as I could tell, he wasn't there. Which was when it hit me, and hardly daring to believe what I was thinking, I walked up the stairs, across the landing and into Harley's now-empty bedroom.

The breakfast tray lay untouched exactly where I'd left it, her night clothes were piled in a small heap on the floor and on her bed, there was a scrap of paper from an exercise book, on which she'd scrawled precisely four words: 'Don't look for me.'

There must still be sufficient time to catch up with her, I thought, rattling down the stairs and putting the front door on the latch. That slamming door she wouldn't have expected had given me precious, precious time. But she must have already factored it in, knowing there was a chance it would have alerted me, because a frantic dash up and down the street produced nothing. Whichever direction she'd gone in, she'd obviously hot-footed it away.

Five minutes later, I was on the phone to the police. *Though should I be?* I thought as I waited for an answer. Should I have called EDT first? Because past experience had taught me that this particular call would last quite a long time. They would have to go through a missing persons form with me and they were very, very detailed. What if I was holding up something important by not getting the report onto the social services system first? Did it differ from the norm with twenty-eight-day placements? It was too late now, of course, and common sense told me that in the grand scheme of things it wouldn't really matter. The important thing was to tell *someone* and get the search under way.

I learned two things during the course of that first phone call. Basic rookie errors. One was that I really ought to go through a foster child's clothing when they arrive – even a child who doesn't ever get dressed or changed – so that I could at least give some description of what clothing they might be dressed in. And second, that until it happens to you, you have no real understanding of how utterly helpless a person feels when told to stay home and simply wait for a phone call or a knock at the door. Which, frustratingly, was how I already anticipated this phone call would probably end.

But it wasn't as if it would make sense for me to go out in my car to look for her, because if I was out and she returned home, she wouldn't be able to get in.

Though would she? Or was she off to try and kill herself? I suspected yes. I know those four words – *Don't look for me* – don't seem that ominous, but in this situation they sent a chill down my spine, and as I paced the floor with my phone trying to answer the dispatcher's questions, I couldn't help wondering if Harley was out there somewhere intending to really harm herself, or whether, anxious not to be interrogated further about her sister, she had just run away. The police, perhaps based on the law of runaway averages, seemed to be thinking the latter. Had we argued? Had I upset her? Was there some unresolved tension?

I explained her history of suicide attempts and justified my lack of background knowledge by telling them she had only been with us for a few days and this, thankfully, seemed to put a different spin on things.

'Okay, Mrs Watson,' the dispatcher said, 'the call has gone out to all officers in the area and rest assured, Harley is being treated as a priority. It's a shame we don't have a better description to go on' – ouch! – 'but at least we have a general idea of what she looks like and her number, which might be helpful if it comes to it. Do you have any idea of where she might have gone?'

'She's not from around here, so she doesn't know the area at all,' I said. 'At least, with what little knowledge I have of her, I don't think so. I don't even know which direction she took, sorry.'

A chilling thought suddenly entered my head. 'Oh, but if it's any help, the last time she did something like this I believe she went to a bridge over a motorway. I don't know if that's something she's done regularly – again, I'm sorry – but it was where she was found last time. It might help concentrate any search?'

'Maybe it will,' the dispatcher said, even though privately, I doubted it. How many motorway bridges were there within running away distance? A lot. 'Anyway, you just sit tight,' she added. 'We'll be in touch immedi-ately if we find her.'

If. Not when. I made the call to EDT next, following the usual procedure, and giving much the same answers as I had given to the police. I then phoned Tessa, who had clearly heard it all before.

To her credit she tried to reassure me that it wasn't anything I had done or not done. 'This is simply how it goes,' she said, 'and you can do nothing else but wait. But be reassured – they always find her. If she ends up somewhere and isn't found, she simply takes herself off to somewhere she's confident she *will* be spotted. It's a bit of pattern with her, unfortunately.'

I tried not to read anything into her rather tired tone of voice. Oh, but how I wished I'd known more before we'd taken this girl on. I had visions of our twenty-eight days being followed by her being moved on for another twenty-eight days, then another, then another, then another … with Harley leaving a trail of traumatised, angry, impotent foster carers in her wake. Perhaps Tessa had been right. Perhaps Harley was 'playing games'.

Lastly, I called my link worker, Christine Bolton.

Christine was less matter-of-fact and understood how I was feeling. 'You poor thing,' she said. 'See? This is *precisely* why I'm not a fan of this type of placement. How the hell are you meant to get to know a child in such a short time, let alone do any meaningful kind of work with them?'

'Tell me about it,' I said as I stared bleakly at my pile of ironing. 'Especially if she's not even here. And even when they do find her, what then? Am I meant to keep her under lock and key to prevent it from happening again?'

'Unfortunately not,' Christine said. 'We both know you can't do that. I know if it were your own child that's exactly what you'd do, but, well, you know as well as I do that it's a violation of her rights.'

Her right to *kill herself*, if she decided to, basically. Yet she was no longer sectioned. Could not be legally contained. 'I know,' I said, sighing. 'It's just utter madness. She gets brought back home and then what? Nothing changes.'

'All you can do is what you've just done, Casey. Make those calls and record the incident.'

Do the admin, in other words. Leave the life-or-death stuff in someone else's hands. God forbid we were caught 'violating her rights'.

Rights she exercised for the rest of the day. My instinct was still to go out in my car and trawl the streets for her – well, the local road bridges – but as there was still a possibility that she might return home I knew procedure dictated that I should really stay put. Mike did, though: even if he could barely recall what she looked like (he'd really seen that little of her), he knew procedure in the Watson household was at least to do *something*, so, while Ty stayed at home with me, to keep me off pins, he was just walking in after a long hour of bridge-crawling when the police finally called.

And with unexpected and rather unwelcome news. It transpired that Harley had been taken off the missing persons list as long ago as 1 p.m. – roughly the time when she rocked up at a local police station and told the officer on the desk that she was scared of us. That if they informed us, or social services, and they forced her to return to us she would simply run away again at the first opportunity.

'She was in a bit of a state,' the officer explained. 'And you know how it goes. Protocol means that we *had* to take her at her word and try to establish if there was a reason she was scared to go home. She also demanded that she be seen by a CAMHS (Child and Adolescent Mental Health Services) worker – she reported that she was feeling suicidal – and a doctor arrived here an hour ago. It was only then that Harley admitted that she did have a safe home to go to, and she retracted having said she was afraid of you. I'm so sorry you've been put through all this worry, Mrs Watson. And now I have to ask you – are you prepared to have her back with you?'

To which I could have said no. A thought that did cross my mind – *scared* of us? Really? But, morally, ethically, did I really have a choice? This was no ordinary child and these weren't ordinary circumstances. So, despite my conflicting emotions, I said the right thing.

'Of *course* she can come home,' I said. 'We've all been worried sick. Tell Harley she needn't be scared about anything. And that we don't have to talk about it – about *anything* – if she doesn't want to. I just want her home and to know she's safe, that's all.'

When I put the phone down, both Mike and Tyler were staring at me, shaking their heads in unison. 'We don't have to *talk* about it?' Mike said. 'That's just great, Case! So she can cause all this mayhem, and then slip back into the house unnoticed, and simply go back to bed again, is that it?'

'We don't have a choice, Mike,' I said, though I felt and understood their frustration. 'Look, we can let this girl churn us up and stress us out to the max, or we can just do what we've been asked to. Provide her with a home for twenty-eight days and that's that.'

Even as I said it, I realised how silly I sounded. Like I could ever do that. And Tyler clearly thought the same.

'That's that, Mum? Yeah, *right*.'

Chapter 6

As Mike had predicted, Harley didn't say a word as she was escorted back into our house that evening. Not to us, anyway. The two police officers who returned her had her sort of sandwiched her in between them, I presumed so they could thwart any attempt to escape.

'Here she is, safe and sound,' the female officer said, a bit too brightly. She looked down at Harley, who seemed tiny between these two towering coppers. 'Do you have anything you'd like to say to Casey and Mike?' she asked her.

Harley didn't look up. Instead she shook her head and mumbled. 'Can I go to bed now *please*? I'm so tired.'

The officers looked slightly embarrassed and I guessed they might have given Harley some sort of talking to in the patrol car; suggesting that she might like to apologise to us for all the trouble she'd caused. And had assumed she would. But then, they didn't know her, did they? Not like I was beginning to. I stepped in to fill the awkward silence.

'That's okay,' I said smiling at the officers and then at Harley, 'I'm sure you're shattered after the eventful day you must have had. Go on, up to your room then and I'll bring up some snacks and a drink in a while, just in case you can manage them. No worries if you can't.'

I could almost feel the scorn emanating from Tyler as he chipped in, 'Well, it's good to see you safe and sound, Harley, but, if you'll all excuse me, I think I'll do the same and retire to *my* room. Snacks and drinks would be good, Mum, if you're doing them anyway.'

I felt my cheeks redden as the female police officer gave him an old-fashioned look. 'Okay, love,' I said as Harley shuffled past me – quickly, so she could beat Tyler to the stairs.

'Well, then,' said the male officer, once both the teenagers were out of earshot, 'we'd better get going. No rest for the wicked, eh?' And, almost as if designed to illustrate that very point, his radio began to crackle: a dispatcher, with another crisis for them to get to.

'Thank you *so* much,' I told them, as they turned to hurry back to their patrol car. 'And I'd say goodbye, but perhaps it should be *au revoir*. This isn't the first time Harley's done this,' I clarified, in response to the female officer's raised eyebrows, 'so it might well be that this isn't the last you're going to see of her. But fingers crossed, eh?'

And I did actually cross my fingers when I said that, but as I shut – and locked – the front door and returned to Mike in the living room, I doubted it would do a lot of good. I just had a hunch that this departure was going to be the first of many. Just the way she'd been, as if this was just what she *did*, her form of protest, almost, and the sooner we accepted that and let her be, the better. Let her die. Yet she hadn't actually killed herself. Again.

In contrast to my own mood, Mike was thinking less about the philosophical than the practical. 'So,' he said, 'what now? Do we lock all the doors and windows and hide all the keys? It hardly seems fair to Tyler to make our home a fortress.'

'Of course not,' I said. 'I mean if she's going to go, she's going to go. And the way I look at it, better she leaves by the front door than something more drastic, like leaping from a window or breaking her leg in order to leave.'

'I suppose,' he said. 'But, bloody hell, Case, this just all feels all *wrong*.'

And he was right. And so began a week from hell, starting with the very next morning.

On this occasion, however, she actually told me she was going. I had just finished chatting to Riley on the phone after breakfast. We'd made plans to get together and order some new baby things for Kieron and Lauren, and I'd just disconnected when Harley walked into the kitchen and asked for a glass of water.

She had brushed her hair and was wearing clothes I hadn't seen before. Black jeans and an oversized grey Disneyland hoodie. I wondered where she'd come by it, who had bought it for her. Because, from what I knew of her and her mother's situation, there was no way she could have been there. Though it had clearly seen better days so perhaps it was a hand-me-down.

'You don't fancy anything else?' I asked hopefully. It was gone 10 a.m. and, at least as far as I knew, she hadn't eaten anything since returning home the night before. 'Maybe a piece of fruit or some cereal?'

Harley shook her head and stared intently at me for a few seconds. 'You do know that I *will* kill myself, don't you?' she said.

Her tone was matter of fact, almost chatty, and I thought carefully before answering, conscious of not wanting to break this slender thread of communication. 'I know that you tell me this, sweetie, and I know you are being sincere when you say it.' I paused for a moment. 'I just hope that somehow you decide that there is another option, realise the world is not as horrible as you think it is.'

Harley smiled but it was a smile that didn't quite reach her eyes. 'Then I don't know what to say to make you believe me,' she said, 'but you should know there's no point in trying to feed me, or nourish me, or whatever it is they're insisting you must do. No point at all. I am sorry, though,' she added, presumably seeing the dismay on my face. 'They shouldn't have brought me here. You shouldn't have to be put through all this.'

I'd turned on the tap and, now it was cold enough, I filled up and passed her a glass of water. 'It's not putting me through anything, lovey,' I said as she took it. 'I mean, of course it's upsetting to know you're hurting and we can't help you, but Harley, it's our job, and it's a job we love doing. I just wish we could ... wish you'd let us at least try to help you through this, that's all. Get you back to your mum. To your own home.'

Harley took a sip of water and put the glass down on the kitchen worktop. 'I have no home,' she said. 'Not anymore. And you can't help me, either,' she added. 'No one can.' She sighed and shrugged. 'Look, I know you have to do what you have to do, but I'm going out for a walk. I need to get out of here for a bit.'

Here we go, I thought. My stomach immediately started to churn. 'So how about I come with you?' I suggested. 'I quite fancy a walk myself.'

Harley looked at me with an expression that could almost be read as pity. As if resigned to the fact that I *really* didn't get it. Then she shook her head. 'I'm going alone,' she said, before turning around and walking out again. 'Please don't worry about me,' she threw back over her shoulder.

As if. I glanced up at the clock and followed her into the hall, where she was already opening the front door. 'Harley, love, I have to give you a time to be back.

It's coming up for ten thirty now, so shall we say one o'clock latest?'

In answer she shrugged, but as she now had her back to me, I had no way of telling if it was a shrug of acceptance or just the visual equivalent of 'whatever'. 'One p.m., then,' I said. Then, as she started down the path, added, 'Harley, be back by then or I will have to report you missing again, okay?'

I watched her go then got back to the job I'd been doing, which was a sort-out of a big bag of various baby items that I'd stashed away for Kieron once Dee Dee no longer had any need of them – they were chronically short on storage space. And as I sorted through the tiny baby grows and vests and bits of cot bedding, I wondered where Harley was, and what was going through her mind. She was no less unknowable than she had been the first day she'd come to us, but she had apologised, hadn't she? About what 'they'd' put us through with her. I could only hope I might have appealed to her better nature.

As if, I thought again, as the clock hands moved round. The girl was seriously mentally ill. Well, the way *I* defined the term. Still, all I could do was keep trying to communicate. '*Hi, sweetie,*' I texted, when it got to twelve thirty. '*I hope you're okay. It's time to be making your way back home now. See you soon, Casey x.*'

Then, at twelve fifty: '*Are you almost home, love? Casey x.*'

Then, at five past one: '*Harley, please reply or I have to report you as missing. Casey x.*'

Let Me Go

All my messages remained unread, however, so at a quarter past one I did what I was paid to. Truth was, her data could have been all used up – I assumed social services were providing her with pay-as-you-go vouchers or some such – so I wouldn't then know if she'd read my messages for certain, but I had to assume she hadn't. So, I spent twenty minutes on the phone to the police again. It made no difference that I'd answered exactly the same questions, and in exactly the same way, as I'd done only the day before. The whole procedure had to be gone through from scratch again. Full description, reasons why I considered Harley vulnerable, assurances that no disagreements or arguments had taken place, and a detailed report about exactly what had happened immediately prior to her leaving the house. And at least this time I was able to describe what she was wearing.

'So, in your opinion, Harley is in grave danger and is at risk of harming herself?' the officer on the phone finally asked me.

I had to say yes to that, of course, because even if I thought she wouldn't go through with it, I had to report what had happened, and been said, and she had told me that she intended to kill herself. Next, I had to call EDT. Though, because being daytime, it wasn't 'out of hours', I could only leave them a message, it was important that the call was at least logged. I then called her social worker, Tessa, who was blitheness personified. Which, given how wound-up I was constantly feeling, was beginning to get on my nerves.

'Oh, she'll be back,' she said. 'Either that or she'll end up in custody somewhere while they decide what to do with her next.'

Which wasn't terribly helpful. 'I've no doubt that's true,' I said, 'but tell me, how is any of this actually helping her? You know, the being with us for twenty-eight days and this constant run-around with her. How on earth does this leave any time to do any kind of work with the poor girl? Her, or her mother, for that matter.'

'We can only do what we can do,' was her answer.

'Yes, I know that, but I'm serious. Do you genuinely think enough is going to change in the next two and a half weeks that you can just pick her up and take her home to her? From what she's told me she doesn't seem to think she even *has* a home – not anymore. And with her setting off all the time, telling us she is planning to kill herself, can you, in all conscience, risk returning her to her mother? Assuming she even wants to go home, which is not the vibe I'm getting. And that's assuming her mother even wants her. Which is not the vibe I'm getting either, to be honest,' I finished.

'What can I say?' Tessa answered, after a short digestive pause. 'I don't *know*. All any of us can do is hope.'

Great, I thought. There was no master plan here, just hope. As if that alone could solve everything. And though Christine, who I phoned next, at least offered sympathy, I knew that she had no answers either. I could only wait and that was exactly what I did. For the rest of the day, through Tyler coming home and going out again, through Mike getting home and us having our tea – though neither of us felt much like eating. It was one thing to accept that there was nothing we could, or even, according to protocol, should do. Quite another to just 'get on' and not worry.

So we worried. And continued to, right up till gone eight that evening, when we eventually got the call we'd been waiting for.

'It's PC Donalson,' the caller identified. I put him on loudspeaker so Mike could hear. 'Is that Mrs Watson? I'm ringing regarding Harley,' he went on. 'Are you okay to talk?'

'You've found her then?' I asked, after confirming who I was. 'My husband was just about to have a drive around the neighbourhood.'

'Wouldn't have done much good,' the officer said. 'She's been admitted to a mental health facility, I'm afraid. We've had to section her for her own safety.'

I asked how it had all come about and the officer explained that units had been cruising around looking for Harley, and while PC Donalson was out and about he got a call saying that a member of the public had phoned in to say they had found a young girl on the railway lines with some kind of ligature around her neck. He had gone to the scene and as Harley had started to kick and fight, he had initially arrested her and taken her to the station.

'A ligature,' I interrupted, 'as in something to strangle herself with?'

'Yes, a ligature,' he confirmed. 'Apparently she had tried to hang herself in some public toilets but fortunately the earphones she'd used snapped before any real damage was done.'

'Oh my God! Is she alright?' I asked. 'Are they keeping her in?' If I'm being perfectly honest, at that point I wished – and hoped – that they would be.

But, of course, this wasn't to be.

'She's fine,' PC Donalson replied, 'but in answer to your other question, I'm stunned to be honest, but no, they aren't keeping her. They want you to go and pick her up.'

Mike was understandably angry after I put the phone down. 'Nothing wrong with her, they're saying?' he barked. 'A *ligature* around her neck and wandering on the railway lines and they think there's nothing *wrong*? I swear, Case, the world's gone bloody mad! Why aren't they seeing that she needs professional help?'

I shook my head. Truth was, I couldn't understand it either. Yet again, the doctor at this new facility had, after spending an hour with Harley, decided that her problems were 'environmental' and that she didn't have a mental health issue. I picked up my bag and slung it over my shoulder, while simultaneously wriggling my feet into ankle boots and bringing up the maps app on my phone.

'Well, that's by the by,' I said. 'They are expecting us to collect her so that's what we'll have to do.' I inputted the postcode the police officer had given me. 'According to my phone we should be there in forty-five minutes so come on, love, sooner we're there, sooner we can get back and relax.'

'*Relax*?' Mike looked at me aghast as he picked up his car keys. 'Chance would be a fine bloody thing!'

I wrote the necessary emails from my phone as we travelled. One to Christine, the other to Tessa, updating them on events and asking them to check in with me the next day in case there was anything else to report. It at least filled time I'd otherwise have spent working myself up into a lather of anger and frustration. Or even having a pointless argument with Mike about how ludicrous all this was – which would have got us precisely nowhere.

It was almost ten by the time we got there, the car park all but empty and almost no one around; not those with the liberty to be out and about, at least. And of the people inside we could see nothing either; squares of light fell uniformly on the grounds and the car park, but even the first-floor windows – where the wards began, I guessed – were too high for anyone to see in.

Unlike the place we'd picked Harley up from originally, this building was more like a normal hospital to look at, but as soon as we were inside, we could both tell immediately that it wasn't quite as 'normal' as it appeared. There were buzzers and intercoms going off all the time and security was almost prison-like – it was everywhere. You couldn't even get in an elevator, let alone ride one, without first speaking to someone on an intercom.

The only thing that was definitely the same as the last place was the conversation we had with the psychologist who was discharging her.

'So the problem is environmental, Mr and Mrs Watson,' he explained to us, putting the kind of emphasis on the word 'environmental' that you'd find yourself doing if you were explaining it to someone who spoke only a modicum of English. And what was going on here? Had every health professional in the land been sent the same memo? 'And as a mental health centre,' he went on, as if we hadn't grasped that fact yet, 'we can't really offer any treatment for Harley on that basis. I'm sure you're aware that the young people we treat here have recognisable, diagnosed illnesses. And looking at Harley's records – and having spent some time with her, of course – she just doesn't fit that category. I'm so sorry.'

I bit my tongue. I wanted to yell, *so what does she have to do to be classed as ill then? How seriously does she have to harm herself to be taken seriously?* But I didn't. I thanked the psychologist for his time – Mike confined himself to nodding and I could almost hear how hard his teeth were gritted – and we went and met Harley in the next room.

She looked up at me dolefully, then rose from her chair. 'Come on, sweetie,' I said. 'Let's get you home.'

Chapter 7

I woke up the next morning fuming. When we have a challenging child in, I wake up in all sorts of moods. Sometimes determined, other times weary about what lies ahead and sometimes pragmatic, just accepting that I must go with the flow, prepared for whatever the day might bring.

But today I was in the unlikely position (at least for someone with my sunny disposition) to wake up and realise I was cross – very cross – before I'd even got out of bed. I felt wired, angry and intent to set right all the wrongs that had kept me awake until the small hours.

In short, I was on a mission, fuelled by fury. I was furious with the doctor at the hospital and I was furious about the lack of progress, but mostly I was furious with Tessa. Actually, no – mostly I was furious to have been put in a situation where I felt I needed to tear a strip off a social worker. They were my colleagues, after all – we batted for the same team. We were both in the business of trying to make children's lives better. Yet, from the get-go, that was not how things felt. So I threw on my dressing gown, went downstairs, fired up my laptop and, before I could talk myself out of taking such action, sent an email to Tessa, asking her to phone me as soon as possible because I needed to speak to her as a matter of urgency.

In my whole career I had never had cause to tear a strip off a social worker. In fact, it would never have occurred to me, except in the heat of the moment, to instigate such a confrontation – far from it. I'd been brought up to see any professionals – be they doctors, or nurses, or police officers, or school teachers – as existing, for right or wrong, above my 'station'. Certainly people to be listened to and respected. A silly thing to admit, perhaps, as a middle-aged woman, but I had that knee-jerk respect for those with more education than I had – and this was true even when I worked as a behaviour manager in a high school. Didn't matter what good work I did, or how much the head bigged me up – a part of me was still the little girl who knew her place and, for good or ill, that sense would, I knew, always stay with me. Of course, since I'd been fostering the list had grown too – social workers, link workers and anyone called 'manager' were now all added to the list of people who I believed I should kowtow to, not least because they all tended to have letters after their names.

But not today.

Let Me Go

Which didn't stop me feeling ill watching Tessa Halliday getting out of her car an hour and a half later.

I'd yet to speak to her. She'd emailed back – *I can be there for ten thirty* – and in the intervening time, Harley holed up in her bedroom, as usual, I'd had to re-clean all the surfaces I'd already cleaned once, just to take my mind off the way I was quaking. But there was something about the way she was walking up my path – as if she didn't have a care in the world – that brought my anger to the fore once again.

Which was why my tone was curt as I said good morning and showed her in. But she seemed not to even notice.

'Will Harley be joining us?' she said pleasantly, as she took off her jacket.

'I doubt it,' I answered. 'She hasn't left her room since she was brought back last night.'

'Brought back?'

'Did you not see my email?'

Now she did at least look slightly flustered.

But she rallied. 'I saw your email about wanting to see me. I haven't caught up on yesterday's. I haven't had a chance yet,' she added pointedly.

'Well, she ran away again. Tried to hang herself. Can I get you a drink?'

This appeared to be a game changer. 'A weak tea,' she said, feebly.

Weak tea. It figured. 'Milk and sugar?'

'Plenty of milk and just half a sugar, please.'

Of *course*, I thought, pettily. Weak tea, watered down even further, and sweetened. But when I returned to the dining room some sort of sea change had occurred. She had obviously worked out I had some sort of issue, and having done so, she was ready to fight her corner.

She'd also been checking her emails.

'Look,' she began, putting her phone down to accept the revolting beverage, 'I can tell from your emails that things aren't progressing as you'd like but, you know, Casey, these kind of placements are *always* like this. Twenty-eight days isn't a long time to get much of substance done – in fact we're very limited in what we even *can* do. I'm not sure what it is you are expecting to happen, other than the work we are already doing. Which we *are*,' she added, 'even if it is in the background.'

'That's just it,' I said. 'Can you elaborate on exactly what *is* going on in the background, please? Because I certainly haven't heard anything about it.'

Tessa shuffled uncomfortably on her chair before answering. 'Well, we've tried to engage with Mum, to do some work there, and …'

'So you *have* engaged with Mum then?' I interrupted. 'As in you've actually met with her and done some kind of preparatory work?'

'Well, no, not exactly,' Tessa replied, looking more uncomfortable by the minute, 'not yet. But we've tried to. We've got her on the phone and made appointments, but so far she's failed to attend them. And though we haven't as yet been successful seeing her at home—'

I was flabbergasted. 'Hasn't anyone even been *round* there?'

'Of *course* they have.' She looked tetchy now. 'But if she won't let us in there's not a lot we can do, is there?'

So much for things going on in the background. So much for Mum working with social services so she felt able to have her daughter back again. This was bad news indeed.

'So what happens now?' I asked.

'We keep trying. What else *can* we do?'

I suspected she was anticipating that my answer would be to agree with her. And in other circumstances, in other placements, I probably would have. Because there is absolutely no point whatsoever trying to force a parent who categorically doesn't want a child, and isn't fit to look after a child, to take them back. It would be putting the child's wellbeing – a child you'd already taken from that parent – at risk. Perhaps even putting them in further danger.

But this wasn't that. I'd been told – and in no uncertain terms, either – that the plan was, and always had been, for Harley to be returned to her mother. I was fuming so much by now that I was fearful for my soft furnishings.

'What you can do,' I pointed out, trying hard to keep my voice from getting shrill, 'is be honest with me! I'm sorry, Tessa, but it's *not* good enough to tell me your hands are tied, not in this case. I was asked to take on this child with a very clear remit. That the priority was to work intensively with both parties to try and get them to a place where they can be quickly reunited. I'm not seeing that happening with Harley and now you tell me it's not happening with her mother either. So what the hell *is* being done here?'

'I can see you're angry, Casey, and I can only apologise. You're absolutely right about what was meant to happen, but if we can't get in to do that work, our hands *are* tied.'

'That doesn't explain why this is only the second time you've come to this house,' I said, trying my best to remain calm; it wouldn't do to actually lose my temper. 'And only this time because I requested it. Because you *must* know what we're going through here, what we deal with on a daily basis. You're linked into all the emails, I report every day, yet no one seems to care enough to pick up the phone and acknowledge the problem exists, even if it's to give nothing but reassurance.'

She blinked at that, as well she might. Because she should have done, and she knew it. 'Casey, I know this is no help, but this is just Harley. This is what she does – it's a merry-go-round, and until she decides to stop it … well, sadly, it's becoming her routine, I'm afraid.'

So, back to Harley, neatly sidestepping the main point at issue, which was that the girl had been placed with us with no real plan to help her, bar a couple of half-hearted attempts to contact a parent who showed no sign of getting with the twenty-eight-day programme whatsoever. And now they were telling me to just accept that her behaviour – her cries for help – were just her 'routine'. I was almost in tears by now, trying to suppress my anger. 'Merry-go-round? Trust me, Tessa, we're not talking about fairground rides here. This girl has just been returned from trying to kill herself. *Again*. This is no merry-go-round, I can assure you, it's a bloody nightmare!'

Something happened in that moment, something that I'd rarely felt before. At that precise moment, I no longer cared what anyone thought of me. I didn't care if Tessa reported me for being unprofessional, or even if I lost my job over it. I just needed to get it out.

'You do realise that since Harley has been here my son has hardly spent any time at home, don't you? And can you blame him? Because Harley's "routine", as you lightly describe it, involves telling me she wants to die, on a pretty regular basis, and disappearing, equally regularly, to attempt to do just that. Now it may well be that all the professionals are confident that it's just "care-seeking" behaviour, but we're the ones who watched her throw herself out of a moving car, we're the ones who fetch her home again with ligature marks around her neck, we're the ones who wake up each morning not knowing if we are going to find a dead teenager in our spare bedroom. Which is a world away, let me tell you, from writing notes in a case file. That is stressful. *Deeply* stressful. And I'm not saying we aren't prepared to take on these risks – far from it. We specialise in taking in the most challenging children – but what we do expect is to feel as if we're part of a team and that everyone involved is doing their absolute level best to make that situation better, not fob us off and pretend things are happening when they aren't!'

Tessa was looking a little stunned but I was far too wound-up to stop now. 'And please don't tell me you know it won't happen, that she would never go through with it, because you don't know that. *Nobody* does. You hear all the time about accidental suicides – about people, young and old, aiming to simply scare someone into action, but going too far. You can't deny that because we both know it happens all the time!'

Tessa had shrunk back into her seat now, clearly aware that she had no choice but to let me rant on, and when she did speak, her tone of voice was somewhat different.

'I'm so sorry, Casey,' she said, her voice more subdued now. 'And yes, you're right – I *do* read every report you put through, every single email, but I'm ashamed to say that, no, I had no real idea how badly it was affecting you emotionally. I can see now that things are a lot worse than we thought. Is there anything I can do, other than come out and visit more often? Do you need to speak with a counsellor or a support group or anyone?'

'It's not about *me*,' I protested. 'It's about galvanising someone – *anyone* – to get some help and support for Harley!' But, of course, it *was* about me, it was so obviously about me, and despite my best efforts not to, I started to cry. It was as if the minute somebody had offered me a kind word, the floodgates had opened and I felt so stupid, bawling in front of a social worker I'd literally just been attacking.

'I'm sorry,' I blubbed, 'it's all just been a lot to handle and the hardest part of all is feeling helpless to do anything. And it really does feel as if Harley has just been dumped here and forgotten about. Like absolutely nothing is being done to help her.'

Tessa sat up straighter again, as if in more comfortable territory. 'Absolutely no need to apologise,' she said. 'You clearly needed to vent. And now I can better understand how much of a strain you're all under, I shall take even greater steps to see something is done. Which is not to say that we aren't already trying, but I think we were all a bit blindsided, to be honest. You know how these things happen – so often it's all done in the heat of the moment, and when we took Harley on, we really did believe Mum was on board. That she did want to work with us, that she wanted the same as we did. And I promise I will do all that I can with the time we have left to get that back on track. But other than breaking her door down—' She splayed her arms helplessly. 'I just don't know how we actually get her to speak with us.'

'And if she won't? What happens then? When the time is up and nothing has been achieved with her mother, what happens to Harley then?'

'Well,' said Tessa, gulping down the last of her tea and putting down her empty mug, 'the good news is that I can guarantee that it will no longer be your concern,

Casey. You won't have to worry because that is one piece of work that we *are* on top of. A plan B, if you like. Harley will have somewhere else to go when she has to leave here so you won't be in this stressful situation for too much longer. You have my word.'

Is that all she thinks I'm worried about? I thought bitterly once she left. That I might not be able to ship her out and move her on to someone else? Did she honestly believe that if she could remove that worry from my shoulders, I would magically start to *not* worry? If that was the case, then she didn't know me at all. Because if that was the case and she was passed on, still on her 'merry-go-round' of suicidal impulses, then I didn't think I'd have a decent night's sleep ever again.

Chapter 8

Another day, another mood – this time a grey one. The more I thought about it, the less I felt all my ranting had achieved. I felt a bit like a plane that wants to land but has been put in a holding pattern, told to just keep on flying round and round the airport – to get on with it until told to do otherwise.

Or ran out of fuel. That's what I mostly felt. Depleted. As grey as the weather, I thought as I drew back the bedroom curtains and searched the cloudy sky for any hint of impending sunshine. Also on my mind was that I hadn't shared any of it with Mike. He was already tired and stressed, and I knew if I shared my altercation with Tessa with him, he'd just add 'being stressed about me' to the load he already carried and he had another full-time job to do already.

So, I'd left it, and now fretted that I shouldn't have left it. We should have discussed it. That was what we did, and we hadn't, and that upset me. As I went downstairs, still in my pyjamas, to make a pot of coffee, I felt something I didn't recall feeling before – the impact of fostering on our relationship. It shocked me. Yes, something had to give when you were looking after extremely troubled children, but please not let it be that.

And it wasn't just mine and Mike's relationship that was having to take a back seat, I'd come to realise. I might have hammed it up a bit for Tessa when I'd spoken about Tyler, but it wasn't so far from the truth. It was all too obvious that Ty was doing all he could to avoid getting involved with this one, which meant he was staying out of the way, and I was missing him. Then there were my own children and grandkids, who must have wondered what was going on – I couldn't remember the last time I'd gone over a week without seeing them and I imagined they probably couldn't either. It was also in marked contrast to the joyful previous month, when they'd be round playing with Annie and Oscar all the time.

Coffee was, of course, only a temporary solution, but for the moment, it worked its usual magic. As soon as I sat down and had a few sips I started to reason with myself. I was being overly dramatic, I told myself: no matter how bleak the immediate future looked, this wasn't one of those long dark tunnel situations, with no predetermined end. It *was* only set to last for twenty-eight days – a very short time, that had already grown shorter – and since when did I follow senseless instructions about kids? Never. So I didn't have to do nothing – I could do what I liked, starting with being a whole lot more proactive and demanding with Harley, unhelpful rules about 'letting her get on with it' or no rules. *We can do this, Casey!* I told myself sternly.

I was just pouring a second cup of my miracle cure when my mobile phone sprang into action.

It was, perhaps predictably, Tessa.

'How *are* you?' she asked. 'Are you feeling any better?'

My gut response was to apologise for making such a scene yesterday. But my head gave it a slap. 'I'm okay,' I said.

'And how's Harley?' she asked next. 'Any brighter this morning?'

As if she might appear suddenly, from behind a cloud, I thought, like the sun. But I knew Tessa was just trying to keep the mood light, after yesterday's humdinger, so I mentally ticked myself off. 'I don't know yet,' I told her. 'I haven't spoken to her yet today. She was sleeping when I checked on her earlier and I imagine she still is. No signs or sounds of activity just yet.'

But it seemed it was me she wanted to speak to anyway. 'I have news for you,' she said. 'Which might be positive.'

'Well, I could definitely do with some of that.'

'At least it might be – not counting chickens – but I've just been chatting to one of the psychologists who met Harley the night before last at the hospital. And though they still don't feel an admission would be beneficial at the moment, they do acknowledge that she is in crisis right now. They feel there may be a variety of reasons for this, but they admit that she does need to be offered some extra help. So, even if she refuses it, they'd like to offer it.'

'Okayyy,' I said. I didn't want her to think she'd ticked that box yet. 'And what would this extra help look like?'

'Well actually, a CAMHS nurse would like to come out and visit Harley. Today, in fact, if that's okay with you? Her name is Sue Timms and she suggested 11 a.m. Does that give you enough time to get organised?'

It was still only 8.30, so for me that would be fine. It was simply a matter of keeping Harley in the house for at least the next two and a half hours. Which, if she was sleeping, was definitely possible.

'I will try not to disturb her until Sue Timms gets here then,' I said, 'and I won't mention the visit, otherwise she might bolt again. So yes, great. And I'll be extra vigilant until she arrives.'

'Well, we both know Harley's record of putting herself in situations where she has to deal with professionals, then not engaging with them, so it's not a given, but it's something at least and you never know, do you?'

I assured her that I didn't. That I'd do my best to keep Harley in situ, and though I knew there was a strong possibility that she'd just refuse to talk, at least it would be an opportunity for me to speak to someone who was familiar with this sort of case. So, if Harley wouldn't engage, then I definitely would. I needed all the tips and advice I could get.

Let Me Go

After pottering about in the kitchen for a while and then nipping upstairs to get showered and dressed, I started to feel a little guilty that Harley hadn't eaten anything for a day and a half – well, at least as far as I knew. I knew I couldn't force-feed her but had no other option than to do what I'd been doing. So, with that in mind, I prepared a plateful of snacks – grapes, a piece of cheese and a packet of crackers, plus a couple of cartons of orange juice – and left them quietly outside her bedroom door. I didn't want to knock and wake her if she *was* still sleeping, and I figured that if she woke, she would most likely need the bathroom, so she'd find her food and drinks then.

It was then just a question of waiting. And with the house spick and span there was little I could do other than camp out at the foot of the stairs. Silly, really – it wasn't like I could prevent an escape, after all. If she got up and came down and demanded to leave the house, I would have no choice but to let her. But by the time Sue Timms arrived, a little earlier than scheduled, I was able to greet her with a smile on my face, knowing the subject of her visit was still upstairs.

'Would you like to go straight up?' I asked her once I'd let her in.

She shook her head. 'I'm afraid I can't do that, Mrs Watson,' she explained, instantly making me feel a bit silly. 'We can't be alone with a child in their bedroom – and not someone like Harley, certainly, given her past allegations.'

That was new, I thought. Had she made false allegations in the past then? If so, about who? The staff at the hospital? Tessa? She certainly hadn't said anything. I was pretty sure *no one* had ever mentioned anything like that.

'Oh,' I said, 'I wasn't aware she'd done that. Was it anything serious?'

As well as feeling stupid, I was beginning to feel angry again. If this child had a history of making accusations against those who cared for her, then I should have been put in the picture about that as well, surely? I thought again of her previous comment to the police that she was scared of us. Would an allegation against us be coming next? I filed the thought away ready for the next time I spoke to Tessa.

Sue Timms followed me through to the dining area and took her jacket off, throwing it across the back of her chair, which, for some reason, immediately caused my skin to prickle. There was something about this woman that I instantly disliked. I wasn't sure what, and she certainly looked the part, in her smart two-piece suit, and with her council name badge hanging on a lanyard around her neck. She looked to be in her mid-thirties and had perfectly groomed, blonde, shoulder-length hair and equally perfect make-up. Was that it, that she looked all *too* professional? If so, I needed to look at my prejudices. But, no, it wasn't that, I didn't think. It was just her slightly snappy manner and something about the way she lobbed her jacket towards my chair, as though she thought she was a cut above and had little time for those beneath her. I might have been wrong, of course – I probably was – but nothing about our ensuing conversation changed my opinion.

'Oh, nothing too worrying,' she said airily, 'but I have heard that Harley tends to stretch the truth when she doesn't get her own way. Fairly typical behaviour from a child with her background. That's by the bye, though. I have met with her before so I do have some kind of relationship with her.' She paused here and looked up at me expectantly before continuing with, 'So if you wouldn't mind bringing her down for a chat?'

'Bringing her down for a chat'? What was she, three? I sighed and left the woman sitting at the dining table while I ventured up to Harley's room, pleased to see that she was obviously awake now as the snacks and drink had gone. I knocked at the door and waited for a moment before calling out, 'Harley, love, there's a CAMHS worker downstairs to see you. Sue Timms, she said she's met you before, can you come down, sweetie?' There was no reply so I knocked again. 'I'm going to come in for a sec, love,' I said, opening the door simultaneously and walking in.

Harley was sitting on the chair in front of her dressing table, still in her pyjamas. 'I don't want to see her,' she said. 'I don't want to see anyone today, thank you. Please?' she added politely. 'If that's okay?' She nodded towards the open drinks carton in front of her. 'I'm drinking the juice, so you don't need to worry, okay?'

I had the strong impression that I'd been recruited as a temporary negotiator in a long-standing conflict between opposing nations. It wasn't an edifying feeling. Still, I had no choice but to play it. 'Can't you just come down for a minute?' I asked, 'just so she can see you're okay?' (i.e. so I could play *my* part in the game.)

Harley gave me a grim smile. 'To check I'm not swinging from the light fitting? Please tell her I'm fine, but I don't want to either talk to her *or* see her, so she's wasted her time. I'm not going down there.'

There was no edge to her voice, but no room for argument, either. And though her flippancy set my teeth on edge – yes, Harley, I wanted to say, that *is* a real concern for us – short of dragging her downstairs, I was not going to budge her. But I'd already anticipated that, so I accepted it without further argument.

'No matter,' Sue Timms said after I went back down and explained. She checked the expensive-looking watch on her wrist. 'I've tried. And that's all we *can* do, isn't it?'

That again. Was it though? Was it really? I was just about to say so, when she said, 'Still, now I'm here, is there anything you'd like to ask?'

I shook my head. 'I'm not sure I know where to start,' I said. 'I just can't understand how a young girl who is constantly trying to hurt herself and threatening to kill herself can be deemed as not requiring any treatment for her mental health. But if that *is* the case, then how can *I* help her? How *do* I stop her from hurting herself?'

Sue smiled the smile of the all-knowing before answering. 'The truth is that you can't. You can do all the practical things – as I'm sure you have already done

– like hiding all sharp knives and razors, locking away bleaches and chemicals, and so on. That way, you are at least doing all you can.'

'I haven't actually,' I said. To which she raised a single eyebrow. 'Though I suppose I could. I just think it would be pointless. Harley's old enough and resourceful enough to work out that if she did want to cut herself, she could do that just as easily with a smashed plate or cup. I lock away tablets and medicines, obviously – I have grandchildren who visit – but, like I said, in my experience, if they feel that compelled to self-harm, they'll always find a way. I had a boy once who cut himself with a spring from his mattress, quite badly, and another who used a shard of broken CD, so …'

'Well, then,' Sue said, standing up and reaching for her jacket, 'it sounds as if you already know what you're doing. You could always change to plastic crockery if it becomes a problem, but anyway,' she added, pulling a card from her bag, 'here's my direct number. Call me, or allow Harley to call me, anytime she's in crisis. It's a 24/7 number – a machine picks up if I can't – but I'll always call back, and if she needs something more urgent, then of course it's 999.'

Marvellous! I thought as I let the woman out and said goodbye. Then stood in the doorway for a moment, gazing out into the street, wondering what the point of the last twenty or so minutes had even been, because once her car had disappeared around the corner it felt as though it hadn't even happened. It might as well not have, I reflected as I went back inside, because what single tiny thing had it achieved? Box-ticking again, that was all. She'd discharged her duty. She'd been able to mark a tick on her slim Harley file and I had learned absolutely nothing. Had received nothing either; not an iota of useful advice.

For all that Tessa was now trying, I really did feel as if she was just being left with me to languish till her time with us was up. But what then? I needed more than just 'We'll take her off your hands again, so don't worry'. What person with a heart wouldn't?

I took a deep breath as I headed back up the stairs. What was she up to up there? What was going through her mind? What could I do to make the situation better? At least she'd taken the snacks, and was drinking, so that was one less thing to worry about. But, once again, when I knocked and called her name, there was no answer. And when I went in, she was back in bed, staring at the ceiling. '*What*?' she said, as I stood there, waiting for some sort of response from her.

'I just came up to let you know that Mrs Timms has gone,' I said. 'Do you feel like coming down? Sit in the garden for a bit perhaps? Sun's coming out and I thought—' But then I checked myself and stopped. Telling her a bit of sunshine might be good for her seemed trite in the extreme. Plus, she was already shaking her head even as I thought it. 'Well, you know where I am,' I finished lamely. She didn't even answer. As if my prowling round my own house while she inhabited it, and ever conscious of her death wish, was a perfectly acceptable state of affairs. As if ticking off the days was the correct course of action and eating off plastic plates was the answer to my worries.

It was insane, I decided as I went back downstairs. Unsupportable. Surely something had to give? Had to change? Maybe the professionals *were* right: maybe Harley *was* absolutely fine and maybe less educated people like me were the ones with the problem. Or maybe something really awful *did* have to happen for them to see things the way I did.

That evening, it seemed something was going to change. But with Harley holed up upstairs – she didn't come down at all that day – rather than running round the streets, it wasn't in the way I'd anticipated. Far from it. Even given the contents of my conversation with Sue Timms.

It was midway through the evening, and Mike and I were chatting about progress, or the lack of. I'd taken more food up to Harley, but so far she'd ignored it. And since I couldn't ram it down her throat personally, there was little else I could do.

Mike disagreed. 'But if she's in crisis – and starving herself must surely count as that, mustn't it? – then surely that's enough for *some* form of treatment. Maybe it's worth giving our own doctors a ring and explaining the situation to them instead?'

'I don't know, love,' I said. 'My guess is that because she'll only be with us for another fortnight or so, they won't want to get involved.'

'But if it's an emergency—'

'Then, as the CAMHS woman said, we have to call 999. But it's not, is it? Plus, I know exactly what'll happen if we call the GP. Even if they do agree to see her, it'll be a week's wait for an appointment at least. Then there's the small matter of getting her there, or getting her to actually *see* a doctor if they do a home visit ...'

'You're sounding uncharacteristically negative, love,' Mike observed.

'Because I just don't see what we *can* do. I've been thinking about it all day and coming back to the same sticking point – that she won't even engage with me, let alone let me try to help her. I can barely get more than two words out of her! Well, unless they're please go away, or I don't want to see anyone. God, it's just so frustrating!'

Mike reached across and squeezed my hand. 'Well, at least, on the bright side, she hasn't absconded yet today.'

And within a second of him saying that, we knew why as well.

He'd just picked up the TV remote to scroll through the channels when, without any warning – we'd not heard a sound from upstairs – the living-room doorway swung open. The hallway was in darkness, and we only had the lamp on in the corner, so we just had the light of the light of the television in which to see that it was Harley (which, of course, it had to be, since Tyler was once again round at Denver's) standing there.

It was enough, though. Enough to see the blood glistening on her. And coming from multiple places – her stomach, arms and legs, it seemed – seeping through the pale satin of her pyjamas and dripping from her hands onto the laminate floor. In the near darkness she looked like the victim in a particularly gruesome slasher movie.

'Oh, good God!' I said, leaping up. 'Mike, will you go grab some towels?' And while he did so, flicking on the light switch as he went, I guided Harley – who seemed in something of a trance – across into the dining room and onto one of the chairs.

'What on earth have you done, sweetheart?' I asked her, as I tried to assess the extent of the bleeding. It felt almost as if she'd been listening in to the conversation I'd had with Sue Timms that morning. Had she? I gently pushed her sleeve up a little and inspected her nearest wrist, which I could see, beneath the smears and trails of blood, was a mess of random puncture marks. 'What on earth did you use to do this?' I said.

'My compass,' she said simply. 'It was in my pencil case,' she added.

Her pencil case, I thought. And she hasn't been in school for how long? I then shuddered as I thought back to my chat with Sue Timms again. All this damage had been caused by a simple maths instrument, of all things. *See*, I wanted to shout, *this is the reality we're dealing with!* But there was no time to rail against blasé women in skirt suits. The colour was draining from Harley's face right in front of me.

'And my coat,' I called to Mike. 'And the car keys!'

Chapter 9

I don't know if I'm getting a bit long in the tooth and jaded, or whether Tessa's use of the term 'merry-go-round' had seeped into my consciousness, but within moments of assessing the seriousness of Harley's wounds, I had something of an unlikely epiphany. There was a lot of blood, yes, but a little blood goes a very long way, as anyone who's had a nosebleed will tell you.

Though Harley looked pale, as if she might well pass out from the blood loss, under a brighter light, now Mike had put the dining-room one on as well, I could see that the wounds weren't actually that bad. Bad, yes, in the sense that she'd do something like that to herself, obviously, but, in terms of losing blood – as in at a rate that might put her life in imminent danger – what she'd done to herself wasn't that serious after all. Yes, there were lots of puncture marks, and in multiple places, but each was just that – a puncture mark, from a sharp but slim instrument. Already I could see blood coagulating around the ones on her wrists, and on her thighs it wasn't so much flowing now as oozing; as long as a wound isn't too big, the body is very efficient in stemming blood flow when it needs to.

But the epiphany wasn't about that. It was about the bigger picture. The fact that she'd come downstairs so quietly and calmly – almost as if she wanted to present herself to us; expecting a familiar train of events to be set in place. And, now I took that picture in, I saw everything differently. She'd hurt herself, no doubt about it (and it must have hurt a lot to stab herself repeatedly with a compass) but it also appeared, now I was taking a more measured view, that she'd smeared a lot of the blood around for maximum effect. In short, she hadn't been trying to kill herself, she'd been trying to create a drama. To stir us into action? If so, this was surely a classic cry for help.

If so, good. But the question was, how best to answer it? She was clearly expecting a big hoo-hah, and for us to rush her to A&E. Which we would have to do anyway – I wasn't about to take any chances, not least with the risk of infection. But if we took away the hoo-hah, the panic, the anxiety and the fuss, would we perhaps break what was a long-established feedback loop and in so doing, perhaps find a way into her mind?

I had no idea if my strategy was the right one (I'd meant every word I'd said about blithely assuming failed suicide attempts were meant to fail) but I was willing to take a punt on it. Mike was hovering nearby and I could tell what he was thinking, even without looking at him. He was thinking here we go again, another night with barely any sleep. Because there was every chance, given that Harley wasn't expiring in front of us, that we'd be low priority, and perhaps stuck in A&E for several hours.

So where I had previously been sitting forwards opposite Harley, inspecting her wounds, I now sat back in my chair. 'You know what, love?' I said to Mike. 'I don't think we need worry too much about this. I mean, we'll need to get these seen to, cleaned and dressed,' I added, half to him and half to Harley, 'but there's no sense us both going, especially as you have work so early in the morning.' I was shaking my head and raising my eyebrows as I spoke, hoping he'd catch on without her seeing.

'But—' he began.

'Seriously, love, I'll take her. It's only ten minutes away, after all. You'll be fine with me, won't you, sweetie?' I added, looking again at Harley. 'In fact, tell you what, Mike, if you could go up and fetch my long raincoat from the wardrobe, we can pop that over Harley so she doesn't catch a chill. Oh, and some socks and her trainers.'

Mike had by this time moved around so he could see my face and I could tell that he was getting with the programme.

'No problem,' he said, heading out of the room and up the stairs, while Harley could only look on, bemused

– or so it looked like – by our apparent indifference to the bloody mess she was in. It was the first time I think I'd seen her looking slightly confused by what was happening. Whether that was a good thing or a bad thing was yet to be revealed, but my instinct was definitely the former.

Mike was back in moments and I set about putting socks and trainers on Harley, who made no move to help but no move to escape her fate either.

'There,' I said when I was done. 'Let's get you out into the car, sweetie, shall we? Take your time – don't want to set you off bleeding all over again. Oh, and Mike, can you record my programme for me, d'you think? See you in not too long, I hope, but don't wait up, okay?' I planted a kiss on his cheek. 'Oh, and remind Ty his jeans are still in the tumble dryer.'

Harley spoke not a single word while we made the short drive to hospital, just sat in the front of the car with me, stiff and upright – a bit like a crash test dummy – though my hunch was that her brain was whirring, wondering what had brought on this marked change in approach from me. But it wasn't until we'd gone into A&E, been booked in (the wait time, amazingly, was only ten minutes and I nearly punched the air) and taken a seat in the waiting area that she finally spoke.

'What will they do to me?' she asked, glancing nervously around and pulling the raincoat tight around her. I hadn't seen her self-conscious in this kind of setting yet. Sullen, yes, uncooperative, yes, but never like this. I had no idea what it meant – perhaps nothing; her psyche was a complete mystery – but I definitely sniffed a change in her.

'Like I said before, I think the cuts are largely superficial,' I said brightly, 'but they will still want to be sure that they're properly cleaned and covered so they don't become infected.'

'I won't need stitches, then?' she asked.

'*Stitches*?' I gave her a look of incredulity that wasn't far from the truth. 'Oh, good lord, no!'

Her expression now was unmistakable. She looked disappointed. Disappointed! And it seemed she genuinely was. 'But they all told me I would.'

'Who told you?'

'On my group chat.'

I filed that one away. 'But how would they know?'

'Because I posted photos.'

I was genuinely stunned now. Wide, wide awake. This was something I hadn't figured on with our solitary hermit house guest. *I posted photos*. Just like that. 'Are you telling me you've posted pictures of your injuries on *Facebook*?'

I was about to go off on one now – not least to myself – about that being the sort of thing that made the internet such a dangerous place for young people, especially troubled teenagers like Harley. But it was very much a stable gate and bolted horses situation, so I stopped myself. And quite apart from anything else, Harley had

a half-smile on her face. '*Facebook*? That's for old people!
No one uses *Facebook*,' she told me.

Typical! I thought, even as I processed what she
was saying. I'd only just got used to using Facebook and
now it was deemed only for 'old people'. Were the
circumstances different, I might have responded with a
wry smile.

'Well, whatever you put it on, you really should-
n't have,' I told her. 'Even with my elderly brain,
I know that self-harm is a private matter and
shouldn't be glamorised in photographs for the world
to see.'

'There's a massive difference, Casey, between self-
harm and attempted suicide,' she retorted. 'Don't you
know *that* with your elderly brain?'

I really wasn't sure what to make of her tone, or her
comment. Because did she really expect me to believe
that she had genuinely tried to kill herself this evening?
Her one constant since she had arrived had been that she
was determined to do just that, but I was beginning to
feel the same as everyone else who'd had dealings with
her. That she had got into this bizarre mental place
where trying-but-not-trying had become something like
a compulsion for her in itself. I just wished I could find
my way into that place with her so I could work out what
to do to try and break the cycle.

What I could work out, however, was that my hunch
seemed to be correct – Harley was sorely pissed off that
her attempt at whatever hadn't gone quite as dramatically

as she thought it would and she didn't like the fact that I was being so blasé about it.

Thankfully, I didn't need to answer, however, as her name was called and we were led by a nurse down a shiny, white corridor, following the coloured strip on the floor that weaved its way around the whole area. I didn't catch the nurse's name, but she seemed my kind of woman, because there was no preamble – she set straight to the task in hand.

'Let's have a look, then,' she said, drawing a curtain around the bed in the cubicle. 'Pyjama trousers and top off, please. You can leave your underwear on and pop this gown around yourself if you wish. Are you alright to hop up on the bed for me?'

I noted that Harley was indeed wearing underwear beneath her pyjamas – as if anticipating that she'd be coming out tonight? Another piece in the jigsaw. Or was it? Like everything with this child it seemed impossible to know. Harley didn't answer her, just silently did as she'd been asked, only wincing slightly as she peeled off the bottoms, where the blood had stuck them to her thighs and tummy.

The nurse seemed not to notice, or, if she did, she seemed unmoved. She was brisk almost to the point of seeming uncaring. But I sensed it was deliberate. Perhaps experience had taught her that being overly sympathetic to serial self-harming A&E attendees only helped reinforce their behaviours. What a complicated business it all was, I mused. I'd seen more than most of self-harmers in my time in fostering and I never felt any less perplexed and saddened by it.

The nurse, though, just seemed keen to get on. Since Harley hadn't answered her first question, she spoke over her, to me. 'So, what did she use to do this, then?'

'A compass apparently,' I said.

'Hmm, and not the north, east, south, west kind, I see.' She examined the cuts closely and then started unwrapping some antiseptic wipes. Now she did address Harley. 'No getting away from it,' she told her. 'This is going to sting. But then if you do this kind of thing often, I'm thinking you'll be used to a bit of pain, won't you? Anyway, I'll be as gentle as I can, okay?'

Harley remained tight-lipped while the nurse started to clean her wounds, though now perhaps more of necessity. Though when the nurse declared she'd finished and gave Harley a short lecture about aftercare, all she got in response was a curt nod. Had this been a different child I might have nudged her to thank the nurse for what she'd done, but this being Harley, there seemed little to be achieved by doing so. A sullen 'thank you' is worse than no thank you at the best of times and it wasn't as if I was training a forgetful toddler. Still, it went against the grain – this was still the same child who'd been so polite and articulate when we'd first met her. To be so stony-faced when being helped must have been an act – an act of will. The question was: why did she adopt this persona? Was she actively wanting to be badly thought of? I'd looked after plenty of kids who lashed out when offered help, but she didn't fit that mould. I didn't get her at all.

'Well, then,' I said, a little too brightly, 'that wasn't too bad, was it? And no need for stitches either, just like I said. Come on, then, let's get that coat on and done up, and then you'll be decent and we can get back home.'

I thanked the nurse for her time and she gave me an understanding look, then it was straight back to the car and in pretty record time. We'd been lucky – we'd not even been gone forty-five minutes. Perhaps Mike might still be up – I hoped so.

'Let's hurry home, love,' I said as she climbed gingerly into the car. I was still conscious of not making a big thing of what she'd done. I wasn't sure why, quite, but I sensed it was derailing her a little, this not having the night panning out as she'd perhaps anticipated. Perhaps it was making her think. 'If I'm lucky,' I added, 'I might still get to watch a bit of TV with Mike.'

Harley slammed the passenger door as she settled into the seat. 'That's twice you've said *home*,' she crossly. 'It's not *my* home, I don't *have* a home.'

So she *was* rattled. And was this a route into a proper conversation? 'I'm sorry, love,' I said as I started the engine and began reversing out of the parking space. 'I know it's hard for you, and it's just what I'm used to saying, but, you know, our home really *is* your home all the while you're with us.' I smiled across at her. 'At least, your temporary home. But of course I know that you must miss your own home.'

'I told you,' she said, 'I don't *have* a home.'

'But you do have a mum, love,' I said, deciding to plough on. I had to take any opportunity I could get, after all.

She didn't reply to this, so I decided to keep going. 'Speaking of Mum,' I said, 'have you been staying in touch with her on the phone?'

I could see Harley's chin just out of the corner of my eye. 'Of *course*,' she said, as if I was an idiot not to already know this. 'Every day,' she added. 'We FaceTime. I don't know why I bother, though, because we always end up arguing. What kind of an excuse is *oh, I can't keep you safe*?'

This was more than I'd ever had from her on the subject of her mother. I pressed on. 'Well, I suppose, in her situation, that's what any mum would feel like if she loved her child and felt she couldn't stop her hurting herself. She must feel helpless, sweetie. Can you see that?'

Harley snorted. 'Oh, she's helpless alright, but not the way *you* think. Look, never mind,' she said, dismissively. 'I don't expect you to understand. And I don't want to talk about her right now, if that's okay.'

Polite again. And it was okay, because I'd fixed on the words 'right now'. Because it might mean she was prepared to talk about Mum at some other time, mightn't it? I clung to that small signal that we might have made a bit of progress. And was happier still to see that Mike had stayed up. As if he wouldn't have, given that I'd texted to say we were done and on our way. Still, I was pleased, because I was feeling oddly distant from my family. It had only been for such a short time but it had felt as if I was in jail. Stuck in all day on my own, Mike off at work, and then Tyler off out most evenings and Harley's welfare dominating both my time and my thoughts.

So I was happy that she headed straight up to her room, for me as much as anything. Keen as I was to try and get to the heart of her, I was tired. 'I'll leave out some milk and biscuits,' I called after her as she disappeared up the stairs.

'Not till you've had a sit down and a coffee,' Mike said firmly. 'All good?'

'All good. Much ado about nothing. Well, not nothing,' I corrected myself, 'but it did all feel very staged. I'm hoping our response – or lack of it – might have given her pause for thought. Though having said that, I hope it won't inspire her to try something more serious. Oh, I don't know. I really, *really* do not know what to make of her.'

'So stop *trying*,' he said. 'Let it go. You can't help her if she doesn't want your help. Here, take your coffee. Let's wind down with a bit of TV, shall we? Put her out of our minds for a bit. Concentrate on our own family for a change. Speaking of which, I had lovely chat with Kieron while you were gone.' He then proceeded to tell me all about what little Dee Dee had been up to and how excited she was about having *her* baby. 'Honestly,' he chuckled, 'I really think she thinks they're having it *for* her! They're going to need eyes in the backs of their heads!'

He planted a kiss on my forehead, then. 'Seriously, love, we really must try to keep this one in perspective. If she won't be helped, she can't be helped and there's nothing to be done about it. Try to detach a bit, okay? We only took her on in a very specific circumstances – to keep her safe, as far as we're able, for just twenty-eight days. And what's left now? We're halfway, aren't we? And, I mean, how hard can it be, right?'

Which was, of course, my line. Which I answered in my head. In theory, it shouldn't be that hard at all.

But theories were exactly that. Just theories.

Chapter 10

Thankfully, my hunch about not making a drama out of a crisis seemed to have been the right one, because for the next three days all was calm on the Harley front. She still wasn't opening up to me – it still felt as if she was present but not present – but I'd heeded Mike's advice about trying to detach myself mentally. I'd keep chipping away at her, but I'd dampen down the drama inside my head.

Though she was certainly involved in relationships outside the home. Though I respected her privacy, and didn't seek to hear any of her conversations, she was clearly having them – I'd pass her room sometimes and hear her speaking to people; whether FaceTiming her mother or chatting to friends, I didn't know. Though did she even have friends? She was such a closed book that I had no idea. Though she wasn't in school currently – how long would that sorry state of affairs continue? – I assumed that, like most young people, she had any number of online relationships, though with virtual or actual friends, I didn't know.

And I resolved not to try and find out. After my moment of optimism, thinking the incident in A&E might be a turning point, she'd barely spoken a single word to me. Ludicrously, since we were sharing a small semi-detached house, she hadn't even *seen* Mike since that night. And as for Tyler, she'd seen him, what, once?

It was as bizarre a set of circumstances as I think I'd ever found myself in, and I still felt under house arrest, but at least her determination to remain holed up in her room allowed me to relax a little and see something of my own family.

Lauren was nearing the end of her pregnancy by now, so on the Friday morning Riley picked her up and they came round for a coffee and a catch-up – though, more accurately, it would be a tea and a catch-up, since, like Christine Bolton (and, of course, inexplicably, as far as I was concerned), they were both dyed-in-the-wool drinkers of the evil beverage.

It was so good to see them, to touch base with my own family, and even better, I saw, as they climbed out of Riley's car, to see that little Dee Dee was with them too.

'Oh, come on in, my little Moo,' I cried as I swooped Dee Dee into my arms, 'and why are you not at school, madam? Are you poorly?'

'I been sick, Nannie,' she announced proudly, 'all over my blankey and my slippers. Mummy said I'm scusting.'

'I did not say *you* were disgusting,' Lauren admonished as the girls followed me in, 'I said your *sick* was disgusting. Honestly,' she added, 'I thought I was going to be sick too. Whoever said morning sickness goes away by the end of the first trimester should be arrested under the Trade Descriptions Act. *Ugh!*'

Slightly regretting my compulsion to kiss my granddaughter's face all over, I put Dee Dee down. 'Oh, God, she hasn't picked up a bug, has she?' I wondered aloud. 'That's the last thing you need at the moment.'

Lauren shook her head. 'I'm pretty sure it's not viral,' she told me. 'Possibly more to do with someone making a potion out of orange juice and milk and sugar while my back was turned this morning.'

For the first time in what felt like ages, I laughed out loud. I glanced towards the ceiling and decided that whatever was going on up there, for the next hour I was going to relax and enjoy my family. After the obligatory cuddles and chit-chat with Dee Dee, I found her favourite programme on the TV – *Horrid Henry*, no less! – and then the girls and I sat around the dining table to talk: husbands, babies, maternity plans, and anything other than the elephant in the room, or at least the one up in the bedroom. But half an hour later and the conversation couldn't help but move on to Harley.

In hushed tones, I caught Lauren and Riley up with recent developments and threw in my own opinions about how conflicted I was about the professionals' view of Harley's attention-seeking (or should I say care-seeking?) behaviour.

'The thing is, Mum,' Riley said, 'they might be right, but they might not be. The news and the internet are chock-full of stories about teenage suicide and how it's on the increase. It's mental health this, mental health that – it's clearly on the rise. Nobody can afford to ignore it.'

That brought me straight back to the nagging anxiety I was carrying with me everywhere. Because I still believed it didn't matter how many times Harley made obviously ineffectual attempts to end her life – the day could still dawn when she decided she'd had enough of practice runs and actually do it, be it inside our home or outside of it. Reminding myself that I couldn't stand watch over her twenty-four hours a day, I resisted the urge to excuse myself and go up to check she was okay. 'You're right,' Lauren added, 'it's getting so that most people our age know at least one family that's been affected by it and we all definitely know someone who has taken their own life.'

Did we? Possibly yes. Probably yes, in fact. It was a thought-provoking and very chilling statement. 'It's just awful,' I agreed, 'and I know you're right. I just struggle to understand it because ten or fifteen years ago, to hear of a suicide would have been such an absolute shock, but now it seems that it's part of our everyday lives. Why? What had prompted such an epidemic?'

I knew the girls didn't have the answer any more than

I did. We were all just trying to make sense of what seemed like a senseless fact.

But perhaps they did. 'It's just the world we live in now, Mum,' Riley said. 'It's social media – at least a large part of it, I reckon.'

Lauren agreed. 'It's the connectedness. If you suffer from anxiety, depression, suicidal feelings, whatever – there's always someone you can talk to, isn't there? And not always in a way that's going to be helpful. If you want to die, there are websites that will suggest how you can do it, ones where people post videos of themselves self-harming, all kinds of horrors.' She glanced across at Dee Dee, chuckling to herself over on the sofa, then stroked her enormous tummy. 'It's a hell of a world to bring a child into, isn't it? Knowing the time's going to come – and it seems to come increasingly earlier – when you can no longer keep them away from that world. It's so scary. But they're such a massive part of children's lives now, as normal as TV.'

'And don't forget,' Riley chipped in, 'that they use them in school all the time now, so it's not like you can keep them away from them.'

Lauren glanced into the living room at her daughter and sighed. 'I fear for my kids, Mum, I honestly do. I want to keep them innocent and oblivious to the horrors they might find online for as long as I can, but even *she* is begging us to buy her an iPad for her next birthday – and she's *four*! And don't get me started on the little ones who come to my dance class. Some already have them. And phones. I mean, *phones*! When they're barely out of nappies!'

I felt for both girls and the complicated stuff they had to navigate. Yet that was how the world worked, so they had little choice. The internet was such a part of everyday life now and everyone was having to adjust to it. I thought about my own parents and the huge stress it gave them when almost everything went 'paperless'; pretty much everything official had to be processed online now and you actually paid a premium for wanting to do anything the old-fashioned way, from insurance to council tax, to income tax, to gas bills. But the implications for young people were just plain scary, as Lauren had said. I had always struggled with the idea of young people being exposed to anything their imaginations allowed, but it seemed it was only just sinking into the collective consciousness that the constant exposure to the Wild West of the internet was detrimental to children and young adults' mental health – and long after that particular ship had sailed. And the longer it went on, the harder it would be to get the genie back in the bottle. If you even could. I could only hope that upcoming generations would see the danger more clearly and take steps to make the online world a safer place.

But in the meantime, while oldsters like me were sharing pictures of kittens, troubled teenagers like Harley were posting pictures of injuries – injuries they'd inflicted on themselves. Was this really the new normal?

I didn't mention that she'd done that. The conversation had taken a grim enough turn already. And, as if to remind us, Dee Dee then called from the sofa. 'What's that, Nannie?' she asked me when I went to see what she wanted. She pointed towards the back of the living-room door. 'Is it blood? Were you poorly too?'

It was part of a handprint – Harley's, no question – which, being where it was, I must have missed.

'Goodness me, no,' I improvised. 'That must be from when I was painting.'

'Did you make a painting?'

'Not *a* painting, sweetie. I was just doing some painting. Some decorating.' Which, *Horrid Henry* having regained her attention, seemed, thankfully, to satisfy Dee Dee.

The girls smiled over grimly. Point made.

Although the morning had given me lots to think about, it actually lifted my spirits a little. Because I realised that it wasn't me taking my finger off the pulse – the world was changing so fast that we *all* struggled to keep up. Even me, as a foster carer who had more chance than most to see the results of society's failings first hand.

With that in mind, once the girls had gone and I *had* checked on Harley, I decided to spend the afternoon doing just that; to complete a couple of online courses to get a bit more up to speed on my current set of problems.

Online learning wasn't a new thing for the fostering service. It had been around for a few years now and was expanding all the time. These days, just by logging into my unique account, I could access literally hundreds of courses. I could then take my pick: either do them instantly online or book in for a classroom-based alternative.

It was an incredible, and incredibly useful, resource, and particularly useful for long-in-the-tooth carers like me, who can often be so bogged down with the nitty gritty of caring that we sometimes forget that fostering is a constantly changing environment and that help, on pretty much any aspect you can mention, is just a click of a mouse away.

It was also ideal for taking a bite-sized approach. Each course generally lasted between one and two hours and once I'd had a sandwich, I was soon engrossed in self-harm and the risk factors of suicide.

So engrossed, in fact, that when my phone went, an hour in, I jumped. It was a call from Tessa.

'I have good news and bad news for you,' she announced. 'I'll start with the good. Which is that Harley's mum wants to see her. Hurrah! We've obviously agreed, and my manager decided it would be best at a contact centre, so the visit can be monitored. We've seen them together before, of course, but that was in the home environment. It will be interesting to observe their relationship in a different setting.'

And after everything that's happened in the interim, I also thought. 'Oh, that *is* good news,' I agreed. 'And the bad news?'

'Is that there's obviously a chance she might not show.' Tessa's tone was flat and I knew she meant 'high chance'. 'She's not exactly the most reliable mother in the world, but we can only hope for the best, can't we? So, can you prepare Harley?' She gave me a time – 11 a.m. – and a date – the day after tomorrow – and a place – a contact centre I'd visited many times before. 'Though as Mum tells me they are in contact on the phone pretty regularly, there's a possibility that she already knows.'

I assured her that I would, just as soon as I'd finished my course, which produced a 'well done you', which felt a tiny bit patronising. Whatever, I decided. It had been a useful, enlightening exercise; even though some of it had made for grim viewing, I at least felt I'd added to my repertoire.

Then it was off upstairs again and see what transpired. Would she be pleased? Or would she flat refuse to go? With so little to go on, I had absolutely no idea.

But it seemed I was about to be enlightened. I was just about to knock when I was stopped in my tracks. I could hear Harley on the phone and, as was often the case, it was on loudspeaker – I presume to keep her hands free because she was doing something else while she talked. I could therefore hear not just her side of the conversation, but the other side as well, and it soon became clear that the other person was almost certainly her mother.

'You're just a liar!' Harley was saying. And in a more animated tone than I had ever heard her use before.

'And you, Harley, seem to forget who's the adult here! Stop speaking to me like shit and just *listen*.'

'I've heard it all before, Mum – *Think before you speak! Don't say anything about anything! Blah, blah, blah!* Yeah, what*ever*.'

'Just *do* it,' the other voice said. 'Do you *want* me put in prison?'

To which there was no answer, just a faint sound of moving, so, as it seemed as if the phone call had been abruptly ended, I walked carefully backwards, like some kind of spy, away from the door.

I wasn't at all sure what to make of it. It had been so brief and so tantalising and I knew one thing I mustn't do was start theorising about it – do my usual adding two and two and making something other than four. But, still, it was a window into her strange and complicated world, and I could only hope that when the day came, her mother would show.

But now was perhaps not the best time to go in and confront Harley, in feigned ignorance that I was telling her something I didn't know she already knew. So I left it till teatime, when I went up with some hot food, and caught her just at the right time – emerging from the bathroom.

'Here's some tea for you,' I said, proffering the tray, which she ignored, leaving me no choice but to go past her and put it down on her dressing table. The room looked exactly as it did every time I ventured in there. Not too tidy, not too messy, just a normal teenage girl's room. But for one thing: there were a variety of clothing items strewn over the bed. Did this mean she was thinking about what she was going to wear for the visit? If so, that was a positive, surely?

She was quick to put me straight, though. 'Oh, and by the way,' I said, brightly, 'we have a visit to see your mum fixed for the day after tomorrow. Did she tell you?'

'*Yes*,' she said, sarkily. 'Though I don't know why she's bothering. It's not like we don't talk every day on the phone, is it? So I expect she's just agreed to it so she can get a gold star from teacher, by turning on her Mum of the Year act in front of you.'

'Not me, love,' I answered, as I returned to the open doorway.

She flopped down onto the bed. 'But you're supervising, aren't you?'

Her tone was so matter of fact that it broke my heart a little. Just the notion that she was going on a visit to see her mother and that the notion of it being 'supervised' was normal.

'News to me,' I said. 'But if that's the case, I'll look forward to meeting her.'

'Don't hold your breath,' she said, 'because you probably won't be.'

Chapter 11

I puzzled over what I knew right through the following day, trying to make sense of what, on the face of it, didn't make any. On the one hand, Harley had suggested her mum would turn up at the contact visit so she could impress social services – well, me, anyway. Plus, she'd pulled out all those clothes which, though it might mean absolutely nothing, might suggest that Harley thought she would too. But on the other hand, and in what was almost the next breath, she'd made it clear that she thought she probably wouldn't. What to make of that in conjunction with the conversation I'd overheard? Say nothing, blah blah blah … say nothing about what? What was her mother lying about, and why was she worried she'd go to prison?

I knew almost nothing about their long-term relationship, obviously, but there was clearly stuff going on between them that was highly antagonistic and at odds with the narrative that I thought I'd been told –

that Harley was depressed and suicidal (which the evidence certainly proved) and that her mother, who was struggling with her own mental health, was simply struggling to care for her daughter as a result. I was shooting in the breeze, I knew, but the dynamic I'd overheard seemed to suggest they were in conflict about something her mother had or hadn't done. Was she covering up for her mum about something potentially criminal? If so, what was it? I knew substance abuse was one of the problems she'd been battling, so was that it? Was there a drug dealer involved in Mum's life? I knew it was pointless assuming anything but I also knew a lot about drug dealers. They were always in the picture – and sometimes in unspeakable ways – wherever a drug-addicted parent was involved.

So when the day dawned bright and sunny – another beautiful early autumn morning – I could only hope against the odds that Harley was wrong and that her mother would indeed be there to do her 'Mum of the Year' act and at least let me observe them together. In fact, I think I was looking forward to the visit more than Harley herself was, because it would at least get us out of the house together. Plus, even if I learned nothing about their past (or their future) I would at least get to see what Mum looked like – something that, for some reason, had always interested me.

But perhaps it wasn't so strange. We had many, many children come into our lives and unless they had photographs – which some did – I always found myself wondering who they most looked like – Mum or Dad, or a mixture – and which one of those parents, personality-wise, was most like the child. It helped anchor a child for me, somehow.

Harley herself was a closed book as ever. Apart from the odd grunt of acknowledgement, whenever I'd checked on her, we'd barely communicated since we'd had the conversation about the visit, and when I called for her to come down so we could set off for the family centre, she looked more or less just as she always looked when dressed – as if she'd picked up the first thing to hand and thrown it on: her usual uniform of skinny jeans and oversized hoodie, accessorised by the earbuds she habitually wore, and which were already in place even as she rattled down the stairs. Pink, now, though. Not white. Were the white ones the ones she'd used to make the ligature? I wondered how many pairs she had. And something else, too. Did she really think the leads on a pair of earbuds would have been strong enough to hang herself with? It was another tantalising glimpse into her complicated psyche, because the answer was 'surely not', surely?

Nothing changed once we were on the road either. She sat in the back – no way would she countenance sitting in the front with me today, for some reason – so I felt like a cabbie with a particularly non-responsive passenger. Try as I might to start up any kind of conversation, she simply wouldn't engage. First, she affected not to hear me, and when I raised my voice enough to render this strategy unworkable, she answered in single-word answers to everything I tried, before saying, 'Look, can we just *not* talk? *Okay?*'

And since I didn't want to get her agitated before entering such a stressful situation, I gave up and turned the radio up instead.

The local family centre was a long-familiar place now, scene of many an encounter – some productive, but, sadly, a greater number not – certainly for the children who'd been here to meet loved and not-so-loved family members while in my care. But then that was the nature of our kind of fostering. For many foster carers, and the children they were looking after, this was a place of hope, and of keeping important bonds strong, so the transition back to their own families could be made that bit smoother; a place of conflict resolution and sometimes happy tears.

No one who didn't have cause to use it would know that, however, because it looked just like a normal, if large, family home – both to make it less clinical and so it didn't stick out like a sore thumb in what was, at least at this end, a mostly residential street. And on a morning like this, with the sun throwing dappled shade from the trees above to the street below, I wondered, as I often did, whether the impression would in any way resemble the reality once we got inside and the 'business' part took place.

We were greeted by a lady I'd met once or twice before, when there with other kids, and who exuded an air of almost palpable warmth; were you to hug her, I imagined you'd be able to feel it coming off her. She was clearly the right person for a job that, given the nature of what went on here, would be freighted with such heightened and often negative emotions.

'Lovely day,' she remarked chattily as she led the way into the waiting room, to which she was gifted at least a ghost of an acknowledgement from Harley, in the form of a 'yes', even if there was nothing in the way of eye contact since she was busy stashing away the earbuds that I'd insisted she remove while we'd been standing on the doorstep.

'Mum's not here yet,' she told us, as she gestured us to carry on through to one of the meeting rooms themselves. 'So just make yourselves comfortable okay? Tea? Coffee? Glass of water?'

'Coffee, please,' I told her. 'Harley, anything for you?'

'Just water,' she said, flopping down into a chair, before adding 'please', not so much as an afterthought, I decided, as to point out, by means of such an obvious gap, that she was doing so only because she knew she was supposed to, according to social rules that she didn't necessarily care much about at that moment.

Rudely, in other words, and I felt myself bristle. Yet again, she seemed determined to make everyone dislike her. And as I'd seen her be polite to a fault, when we first met her, I knew it was strategy as opposed to a lack of manners. But why? What purpose did she think it served?

When the lady left, I turned to her and almost opened my mouth – to remind her that the poor woman was just doing her job – but as soon as I did so, I closed it again. Harley had already picked up a magazine and buried her nose in it, and, besides, what purpose did *I* think it served? So I sat down too, and we waited, and the coffee came, and I drank it, and we waited, and waited some more. I tried once to talk to her – asked her if she was okay, commented that she must be finding the wait stressful – but all I got in response was 'It is what it is', so I shut up then and we waited some more. And when an hour had passed, the lady appeared again, the smile not quite so evident on her face.

She'd been in once – all okay in there? – and now she frowned apologetically. 'I'm so sorry,' she said, 'but we need the room for another family now. You're welcome to wait a little longer, of course, back in the waiting room. If you'd like to, that is …'

Harley stood up then and shook her head. 'She's not coming,' she said. Then, turning to me, 'I told you she wouldn't, didn't I?' before heading out of the door, fishing for her earbuds in her jeans pocket as she went and almost barging the poor woman out of the way.

'I'm so sorry,' I said to the woman, albeit quietly, as I followed. She touched my arm lightly, caught my gaze. Nodded. Given that we'd both been here before – witnessed some version of it, anyway – we didn't really need to say anything to each other, after all.

Let Me Go

I followed Harley back down the corridor, passing the large playroom I remembered, and which was equipped with everything you might find in a nursery school. A room designed for much younger children and their parents, during difficult times, but a lovely, happy room nonetheless. Such a contrast to my current mood. There was nothing lovely or happy about what had just happened.

Having almost forgotten my jacket, and having to rush back to fetch it, by the time I got outside, Harley was leaning against the side of the car bonnet, arms and ankles crossed, eyes closed, face tilted up towards the sun. Tall for her age, she was all angles and coltish limbs; at that point on the cusp between girlhood and womanhood. I wondered what kind of life might be ahead of her, had her father not died. If she'd grown up secure in his constancy and love. If there was any way anyone could make any of this better. To make the sun on her face reach her heart.

I wasn't sure if she was even aware of me in that moment, because she didn't move until I pressed the car remote and it double-bleeped to say it was unlocked. 'Something must have come up, love,' I said as I held open the car door for her. 'No doubt we'll hear all about it, but shall we do something together instead, now we're out? Maybe go shopping or to McDonald's?'

I watched her expression change. To one of irritable resignation. If a face could definitively say 'leave me alone', just by those small tweaks of features, that, I decided, was exactly what it would look like. 'You don't honestly think I expected her to come, do you?' she answered, folding her skinny frame into the back seat again. 'And I really don't need pacifying, Casey,' she added. 'I just need to get back and sleep away the rest of these bloody twenty-eight days! And if I get the chance to end it, I will,' she added, snapping her seat belt into place. 'So no, I don't need taking anywhere, *thank you*. Just back.'

And then what? And then what? I wanted to bark back at her. I had to bite my lip to stop something I'd regret from coming out.

'Right, ma'am, back it is then,' I said.

Which was when she took me completely unawares.

I don't know if it was because of the way I'd called her 'ma'am', or whether she'd already decided to do it anyway, but before I could properly take stock of what was happening, I heard the click of the seat belt releasing and then the rear passenger door – which I was still in the process of closing behind her – was pushed open again, hard, whacking me square in the stomach. I staggered back, and if I hadn't still been holding onto the handle, I'd have probably been laid out on the pavement.

Then, before I'd even properly regained my balance, she'd jumped out and was stomping off up the street.

'Are you alright, dear?' An elderly lady had hurried up the pavement from behind me, having obviously seen what had just happened.

'Yes, yes, I'm fine, thanks,' I assured her, as I regained my centre of gravity. I'd dropped my bag and she bent down to try and pick it up for me, but it was soon obvious that her back wouldn't let her. And all the while Harley was getting further and further away. And the car was facing in the wrong bloody direction.

I snatched my bag up myself, shut the car door and pulled the key back out of my pocket. 'Thank you,' I said to the lady anyway, clicking the remote again. Then nodded towards the direction where Harley was walking. 'Teenagers, eh! What would you do with them?'

She nodded her agreement. 'Oh, yes, yes, you go, dear.'

So I sped off up the road, leaving the lady, I suspected, with the impression that I was the sort of woman who'd raised a daughter who thought it acceptable behaviour to punch her mother in the gut with a car door. But I was not letting her get away, not this time. Sod protocol! I was sick and tired of passively standing by and letting rules about what I could and couldn't do around Harley constantly dominate my day.

In truth, I was sick of letting Harley herself dominate my days. Well, not *this* day, I thought as I broke into a jog to catch up with her. And as I panted along the pavement (I am not built for jogging) it occurred to me that if Harley really did want to escape me, she'd be running right now instead of power walking. Which made me even surer that I was doing the right thing.

The road was mainly residential and, after jogging past some thirty or forty houses, I was approaching the junction with the main road and now only a few metres behind my prey.

'Harley, wait!' I called out then and was gratified to see a slight break in her stride – so, despite the earbuds, she could evidently hear me.

'Harley, for goodness' sake, *stop!*' I commanded, but now she knew I was right behind her, she behaved as if she didn't and even slightly upped her pace.

The heavy traffic at the junction prevented her from crossing and, clearly anxious not to wait for the lights, she veered right along the main road, heading down along a short parade of shops. I quickened my own pace till I was level with her, then did something I knew I shouldn't. Did, in fact, precisely what a million mums of flouncing teens had done before me. It felt like the most natural thing in the world. I grabbed her forearm, pretty firmly, to make her stop.

She jerked her arm free of me. 'Just leave me *alone.*'

'No, Harley,' I panted, 'I will not leave you alone!' Then, buoyed by the fact that she hadn't gone stomping off again, added, 'Look, I know you're upset about your mum not showing up—'

'No, I'm not. I *told* you. I don't *care!*'

'Rubbish!' I snorted. 'We both know that isn't true.'

'I so *don't*! She can do what she likes. I don't *care!*'

'Oh, for pity's sake, Harley, just shut up and listen for a moment! I am so *sad* for you, you know that? More than I think you fully realise. So how do you think *I* feel, knowing all the crap you're going through?' I raised the fingers of one hand and ticked them off with another. 'Sad that you won't let me in. Sad that you won't let me help you. Sad that you're up there in *my* bedroom, feeling terrible, all alone ... Sad that everyone around you seems to be failing you. Trust me, I look at you and I could *weep* at the unfairness of it all!' I prodded my chest. 'That's how *I* feel. So all of your "No, I don't want to talk to you", your "Please don't worry about me" nonsense and your "Sorry to be such a nuisance" stuff – they're just words, which mean nothing to you. And nothing to me either. Except to make me bloody fume. Because I'm human, and I do worry and I *will* worry, okay? I cannot *not* worry about you. I cannot *not* care about you. And let me tell you, if you don't come back with me, and get in the car with me, and come home with me, *now*, then I will do what I should have done in the first place. I'll follow you around, letting you know that, till you do!' I took a breath then – I needed to. And she was gawping at me. *Good*. 'And if that means I'm violating your rights' – I put the words in finger quote marks – 'then they can arrest me. So, which is it to be?'

She'd already removed one earbud and she now tugged out the other. 'God's *sake*,' she said, those pale eyes of hers locked onto mine. '*Okay. Fine.*' Then stepped around me and marched off again, but back the way we'd come.

We'd been standing outside a dry cleaners and there was a sign in the window. It said 'Alterations-while-U-wait'. Which made me smile. Because something *had* altered between us. I knew it. The question was – why the heck had I waited so long?

I turned on my heel and hurried after her.

Chapter 12

It's a mantra I've had cause to use a million times in fostering, but I said it to myself again: Rome wasn't built in a day. When we returned to the car – I kept a calculated two or three steps behind her all the way – she had her earbuds back in and was waiting by the door for me, eyes firmly fixed on the ground, as if making any sort of acknowledgement that I'd won this battle would be a step too far. Which was fine. I didn't speak to her, just whooped away inside. Because it felt nothing short of a miracle.

I also reminded myself of another fostering mantra: that children – *all* children – needed boundaries. *Responded* to boundaries, which was the crux of the matter. Harley might not be one of the hard-bitten children of the system I'd often encountered, who, playing the game, wilfully tried to break any that were given to them at every turn, but she *had* fallen into a pattern and it was beginning to make sense for me.

Finding the pressure building up so much that she had to relieve it – by harming herself, running away, making ineffectual attempts at 'ending it' – and then, having done so, not quite knowing what next to do. And the professionals, constrained by their necessary protocols, didn't know what to do with her either. They couldn't force her to do anything, because the law said they mustn't – since her discharge from the hospital, she was no longer sectioned, and if they were agreed that she shouldn't be (and they all agreed on that one) then what else could they do for her? Just try to instigate interventions that, by the nature of her legal rights, she had absolutely no obligation to engage with. And why would she? Because I had a hunch she was intelligent enough to see things as they were; that all the people around her were there for one reason. Because it was their job to be, nothing more. Which wouldn't alter her miserable world-view at all.

And that was probably how she'd seen me and Mike, when she'd come to us. Just a couple whose job it was to provide bed and board for her. Who'd do what we were asked to because it was our job to. What love and security had she experienced, after all? With a long-dead dad, an absent mother and a sister who'd left her?

She was wrong, of course. We all cared. You didn't choose a career working with troubled children if you didn't care. But it struck me that she needed to see that for herself in the same way my own kids had experienced our love and care, not just in the obvious ways, but in the less obvious ones too. When we freaked out at them because they'd worried us senseless.

What was that saying? That the opposite of love wasn't hate, it was indifference. What had she seen, since being in the system, that was anything like evidence that feelings were involved? She'd seen professional concern, yes, but that wasn't quite the same as being loved, was it? She probably thought – and she wouldn't be a million miles away from the reality – that when all the professionals went home to their own lives and families, they might worry a little about her, because they were conscientious about their work, but they didn't care to an extent that made it truly personal.

So she could sit and scowl all she liked on the journey back home. I whooped. We had finally made some progress.

With Harley's mother, however, clearly not, though. And I had to bite my lip again later on that afternoon when I finally had a return call from Tessa after I'd rung to let her know about the no-show. She just didn't seem to be the slightest bit fazed.

'She doesn't really have the wherewithal, I'm afraid, Casey,' she told me. 'She barely has the get-up-and-go to get herself dressed, I don't think, never mind get on a bus and make her way to a family centre. She was given a travel warrant, by the way, so it's not that she didn't have the money. I just think her own mental health is at rock bottom right now, sadly. When it came to it, she simply couldn't face it.'

'You've actually spoken to her?'

'Yes, I have and she's sorry.'

'Sorry?' I spluttered, thinking back to the phone call I'd overheard. 'I don't think she's sorry. I don't think she ever intended to show up. Did you read my email about the phone call I heard Harley have with her mother?'

'No, not yet, but—'

'Well, when you do you'll find out that she was talking about prison. "Do you *want* me put in prison?" I heard her say those exact words. So perhaps there's a reason she didn't want to meet Harley earlier. And, given everything, wouldn't it have made more sense to have someone go and pick her up?'

'That's not really our job,' Tessa pointed out. Then seemed to backtrack a little. 'I mean, I suppose we *could* look into it, but to be honest with you, parents in this position really ought to be fighting to prove *they* want to make it work, not be dragged there kicking and screaming, but so far all this woman has done is treat this time like a holiday, sad to say. Still, on the bright side, she's promised me that she'll try again, so we've arranged another contact visit for the day after tomorrow. Let's keep our fingers crossed – see how that one goes, shall we?'

Try again? I was as flabbergasted as I was angry. I politely said goodbye, but all the while I was seething. Because in my opinion, which didn't seem to count for much in this case, social workers in this position ought really to be fighting too – to ensure that a twenty-eight-day placement was what it was meant to be. Not just seen as any old port in a storm, which was increasingly the vibe I was getting here, but as a real opportunity to work with both parties, to repair any damage that had already been done and to help put the pieces back together – however tentatively – so they could at least live under the same roof and the child could be released from the authority's care. It was hardly rocket science. And if the case was more complex than that, and the outcome that uncertain, then why go for a twenty-eight-day order in the first place? My agreeing to this whole thing had been predicated on a simple premise – that social services had been at least reasonably confident that Harley was on the mend and Mum just needed a little more time to work with the service so that she would feel able to keep her daughter safe and have her back home. Yet here we were, nearly three weeks in, and despite my intemperate rant a couple of days back, not a single thing had really changed.

Not for the first time, I felt deeply frustrated. I banged my coffee jug down on the kitchen worktop a little too hard as a consequence, which made me crosser still. It was my new rose-gold, thermal, four-cup coffee jug – an early birthday gift from myself to myself. If I broke that it would be all too symbolic of my current mood – that, given the lack of support I was getting, and the way it increasingly seemed I'd been misled, I now fretted that

I'd be just at the point of getting through to Harley when she'd be whisked away to another family of strangers! And even as I attempted to calm myself down with my favourite beverage, the rich, bitter, restorative tang of the hot coffee couldn't disguise the taste of betrayal welling up inside of me. Much as I wanted to help, to do my best, how could I do anything *to* help, given that I couldn't, in all conscience, let Kieron and Lauren down? I had to do as I'd promised and make them my priority, even if that meant having to let Harley go.

Needless to say, the child at the centre of all this remained in her bedroom, determined to sit it out, incommunicado, till something about her situation changed. Or the agony built up and she decided to abscond again. I had no idea when or if that might happen, and since she didn't emerge again that day, I could only do what I'd been doing – taking food and drink up at regular intervals, as if I was in charge of a police station holding cell.

So, two steps forward, one back. That was the way it often worked. Trouble was, we would soon run out of road. Were running out fast – the next time I actually saw her wasn't till the following morning and only then happened by accident. I was in the bathroom emptying the laundry basket when she appeared in the doorway.

'Oh, I'm sorry,' she said, immediately backing up onto the landing. 'I didn't realise anyone was in here.'

'It's fine,' I said. 'I won't be a tick, just collecting all the dirty washing. Mostly Tyler's stinky socks,' I added, wrinkling my nose theatrically. 'I should be given danger money for doing this kind of work, I really should!'

I was rambling because I was just so anxious to strike up a conversation, ideally before she disappeared again. But she clearly needed to use the loo because she remained just outside the bathroom doorway.

'How are you doing, love?' I asked, my arms now full of washing. 'We haven't really talked since we got back yesterday, have we?'

Harley shrugged. 'What's to talk about? Let's face it,' she added, folding her arms across her chest, 'even *you* should now be starting to believe this world isn't for me. God, even my own *mother* can't stand the sight of me, can she? As you found out.' She smiled then. 'Please don't look so sad. You know, it's fine. It really is. When I do leave, I'll be happy to go. *Seriously.*' She moved away from the doorway then, presumably so I'd pass her. 'No more of this miserable existence. No more pain. No more feeling like everything is pointless. Honestly, it won't be sad, it'll be a blessing.'

It felt like the most honest and soul-searching thing she'd said to me since I'd met her and no matter how grim her words were, or how obviously she was standing there waiting for me to vacate the area, I was going nowhere. Her need for a pee was clearly my unexpected opportunity.

'I think you're wrong about your mum, Harley,' I said. 'She must be beyond despair that she can't help you and as a mum myself, I can all too easily imagine how her own mental health must be suffering as a result. How much she's struggling with the whole situation. And she's sorry about yesterday – I know, because Tessa told me – and she wants another meeting tomorrow. They are going to organise a taxi for her this time as well. So, please, love, for both your sakes, can we give her another chance? You want to go home to her, don't you?'

Harley uncrossed her arms and spread them wide, either side of her. '*Seriously*? You *really* think that ...' The arms slapped against her sides. 'Oh *God*, never mind. Fine, yes, okay then, let's all go on another pointless journey while my poor old mother gives us all the run-around. *Great* idea! Fine though. *Whatever*. Now can I get into the bathroom or what?'

I spent the rest of the day going through all the usual motions. Cleaning the house, drinking coffee, catching up with the kids, doing the washing and, of course, delivering trays of food to Harley. And despite it occurring to me often – every half hour or so, to be precise – that I should just stomp up and march in and demand that she talk to me properly, I knew it was pointless. Which made *me* feel pointless. And rail against the whole twenty-eight-day thing, *again*. She should never have been put on it in the first place. That was my absolute opinion. She should have been subject to a full care order from the outset, and given a comprehensive care plan, and even if she sat saying nothing at every meeting, should be regularly meeting mental health professionals, to boot. At least she'd be in a situation that wasn't time limited the way that this was. Would have no 'get out of jail' card to wave in anyone's face, or excuse to stay holed up and close down emotionally.

Yes, when the time came for me to feedback on what I thought about the whole placement, I would waste no time in sticking the boot in. Because I really did feel like a prison officer, with a very simple remit. None of the love, nurturing and emotional wellbeing stuff I was trained for – but as a compiler of endless notes and provider of bloody snacks!

Christine called towards the end of the day – 'Just checking in! How you doing?' – and when I said as much to her (well, the edited, profanity-free highlights) she assured me that she believed Harley's mother when she'd said that she felt terrible and really was going to be there. 'She's so much happier. About the taxi, that is. As I said to Tessa, we really should have arranged that in the first place. But you know how it goes – cuts, cuts, cuts!'

Which made me think of the old adage 'for want of a nail'. And though I couldn't quite recall the rest – was it a shoe that was lost? – it was yet another thing for my increasingly angry journal.

Still, I was determined to remain positive. And it seemed something of my positivity, plus it being another gloriously sunny morning, might have rubbed off as even Harley seemed a little perkier as she climbed into the car the following day. At least, it seemed that way – but it wasn't quite as I'd thought. 'Fingers crossed, sweetie,' I said, as she strapped herself into the back seat. And was rewarded by a little smile as she twisted in her earbuds.

'Yes,' Harley said, 'but no sad faces if she doesn't show, okay? It's just pointless. Because the chances are she won't.'

'Have you spoken to her?'

'Not today, not yet.'

'Yesterday?'

'Yes, of course.'

'And what did she say?'

'That she was sorry. What else was she going to say?'

'I don't know, you tell me.'

Harley made a little 'tsk' noise. 'Casey, her words are worth *nothing*,' she said, echoing the exact thing I'd said to her. 'Don't you *get* that?'

I didn't answer for a moment because one of the things I'd learned in my many years of fostering was that all the cosy absolutes in fiction about mums and dads and love didn't apply in real life. That, mother or not, her words might well be worth nothing, just as Harley had told me. What mattered though was that we find out whether that tragic state of affairs was temporary, potentially fixable or permanent. And whatever the circumstances behind it – and knowing so little about either of them, I couldn't jump to conclusions – the future was key here. If her mother didn't want her daughter back, and was just stringing everyone along, then this whole thing was not only a waste of everyone's time, but only adding to her psychological damage.

Harley was looking at my reflection in the rear-view mirror, I realised, presumably watching my thoughts dance across my face. She sighed. 'Look,' she said, leaning forward a little, 'it is just what it is. So, we go in, we wait for a bit, then we leave and come back. It's just silly going over all the whys and wherefores.'

A strange turn of events indeed. A foster child advising the foster carer on how to accept being let down. By *her own mother*. She really was an oddity and even though she had been careful not to allow us to see much of her, either physically or otherwise, I still hung onto the way she'd reacted when I'd shouted at her; there was something about Harley that I felt I *was* beginning to connect with. It might have been a bit arse about face (she wasn't exactly patronising me, but she was definitely trying to 'manage' my expectations) but she seemed genuinely keen to prepare me. And as it happened, she had read the situation better than any of us. Her mum didn't show up and after half an hour in the family room I felt her hand on my arm. A child's hand. Warm and soft. A hand *on my actual arm*. It was the first time she'd ever reached out and touched me.

'Come on, Casey, let's just go. There's no point in waiting any longer.'

'But—'

'If they ordered a taxi it'll have been at the right time. Honestly, she'll have just not answered the door.'

She had a point, and with little choice, I followed her lead. She was right, clearly. Her mother, anxious not to fall foul of social services, was talking the talk but with no intention of walking the walk. She was happy to talk and do FaceTime, but she didn't want to see Harley, not face to face. I had to accept that *was* probably the truth of it.

As anyone could have predicted, when we got back, Harley went straight back up to her room. It was just so sad, on a day that was meant for being outside, to watch her trudge back up the stairs, to her self-imposed isolation. What scheme could I conjure now to get through to her?

I was sitting at the garden table, mulling just that over a coffee in the sunshine, when Tyler appeared in the conservatory doorway. He'd had a free morning, so when I'd left, he was catching up on sleep. But he was now showered and dressed, ready to go in to do his shift at the leisure centre, but clearly had something to say.

He pulled out a chair and sat down on it. 'Can we talk, Mum?' he asked, glancing up towards the bedroom windows. 'It's about Harley.'

'Course we can. What's up, love? Something new?'

He nodded. 'I didn't know you'd gone at first,' he said, 'so I was knocking at her door – I needed to grab an extension plug to borrow for half an hour and I knew Harley had mine. Anyway, the door pushed open while

I knocked, which was how I realised she wasn't in. So yeah, I went in to get it, but, Mum,' he leaned forward, 'she had her laptop plugged into it, and she'd left it open and on, and ...' He glanced up at the windows again.

'It's okay,' I said. 'The window's closed and the curtains are shut. Spit it out, Ty. I'm guessing you looked, love? Which is fine. Under the circumstances I would probably have done the same. What was she looking at?'

'Not so much looking at,' Tyler said, 'she was fully participating in a full-on chat room about suicide. I mean, not just in general, but lots of people, mainly young ones – well, assuming their profiles were true – all talking about the different ways they had attempted to die, and wanting to die, and planning to die ... and, oh my *God*, it was just mental, Mum! I mean, seriously. It was *sick*. I scrolled through it too, because there was this one guy who I noticed that Harley had been talking to, and he actually said he was going to do it tomorrow. He said he was going to attach a pipe or something to his mum's car exhaust when she was out at work, then take a load of sleeping tablets in the car and just wait to die! Do you think he means it? I can't stop thinking about it.'

'From everything I've read recently, babes,' I said, 'the thinking is that those who talk about it, and tell people their plans, usually have no intention of going through with it, so, Ty, I wouldn't worry too much about it, love, honestly. But hey!' I lifted my mug in a mock cheering motion. 'Welcome to my world,' I said. 'Welcome to the dark side.'

Because if you don't laugh, you cry, right?

Chapter 13

They say, don't they, that we humans make plans, set-in-stone plans, but then the universe, or God, or destiny – which always loves to laugh at us – steps in. And, as a consequence, those plans, however best laid they are, go up in smoke and we are thrown into turmoil.

Which, with Harley, was exactly what happened next. But not before whichever deity was responsible threw a few teasers across our bows first as warning shots.

After the second incident of Mum not turning up to see her, Harley, having outwardly shaken it off as though it didn't matter, retreated even further into herself. Which might seem impossible, given she was in retreat mode all the time, but when you are living in circumstances as odd and extreme as we were, the tiniest differences in atmosphere are very noticeable. It was like having a ghost in the house.

We were now into the fourth week of our limited-time placement and despite my small victory in getting her to come back to the car with me that day, I felt as if I'd done nothing to change anything. And social services still hadn't either. Both Christine and Tessa kept assuring me that things were still 'going on in the background' – meetings and phone calls and discussions with professionals about best next steps, but if that were the case, then I wasn't privy to any of the outcomes. Which made me believe that it wasn't the case, obviously. They were still winging it, in my view, and whatever discussions were going on, I suspected they were definitely more to do with trying to find somewhere else for Harley to go now.

Which I knew she still had to. Because we'd been clear from the outset that I wasn't in a place to hold onto her indefinitely. Much as my heart bled for her, I had to put my own family first. Kieron was an adult now, obviously – and a fine one, and a good father – but he still had his challenges, and he and Lauren still needed my support to help them navigate the enormous changes a new life in their family was going to mean. It wasn't any kind of crisis – they were both beyond excited about the coming baby, and I knew, because of Dee Dee, that they were going to cope okay. But I also knew that my support would be crucial. I could provide a steadying pair of hands – both emotional and actual – as they lived through those early days and nights with a newborn that can derail the most confident and pragmatic of parents.

There was also Tyler to consider, and consider him I must. Though we'd had a reasonably light-hearted discussion (I'd steered it that way) about what he'd seen on Harley's laptop, he'd been mulling things over since and it had obviously shaken him up.

'I just can't believe it, Mum,' he said to me when we were all watching the evening news after tea the following evening. 'I can't seem to get it out of my head that she's up there, in that room, just across the landing from me, getting involved in all that stuff. That she might actually kill herself in *our house*, while we're all *here*.'

'What kinds of stuff did you see on there, son?' Mike asked.

'Stuff I wished I hadn't,' he said. And his tone was a reminder (as if I ever needed one) that our strapping eighteen-year-old had once been a deeply troubled, deeply anxious, very frightened boy himself. 'I just can't stop thinking about the lad who'd planned to kill himself in his mum's car. D'you think he did? I almost want to get onto that chat room myself, just to find out if he went through with it or not.

'And it's not just that – it was the way everyone was, like, properly egging him on. Talking about how he'd be at peace, and out of pain, and all sorts of stuff like that. How he'd finally be happy. I mean, how can you be happy when you're *dead*? I've never seen anything so creepy.' He looked at us both anxiously in turn. 'I mean, do you think he did it? I can't stop wondering if he's still alive.'

At which point I knew I needed to step in, decisively.

'Yes, he will almost certainly be,' I said firmly. Firmly enough that Mike glanced at me slightly quizzically. 'I mean, I can't say for definite, but I am ninety-nine point nine per cent sure. Remember what I told you? Kids who are talking about killing themselves on these kinds of forums are the ones *least* likely to be actually doing it. Not them. The ones who do are the ones who tell no one. They just do it.'

I had absolutely no idea if what I was saying was true. In fact, I made a mental note to do a lot more research into the subject. I could be totally barking up the wrong tree, after all. But instinct told me that I was right. And if I wasn't, so be it. I could correct my world-view later, and Tyler's too, if it came to it. But right now I was concerned with only one thing. That Tyler didn't obsess over and get upset about this too. That he didn't lie in bed at night wondering if he was going to emerge from his room the next morning to find Harley's body being carried down the stairs. It was a deeply distressing thought. We had no business inflicting such horrendous memories on him, even just potentially.

'I think Mum's right,' Mike added, having correctly interpreted my strategy. 'Yes, it's obviously awful to think of these things going on online, and that there are kids trying to persuade other kids to end their lives – it's *horrible* – but if he was dead set on doing it, he'd have already done it is my hunch and sometimes being around others who are egging you on *to* do it turns out to be food enough for thought – to think again.'

Which could have been another load of gobblede-gook, but Tyler was nodding sagely and I could see our reassurances had been a good thing.

'Dead set?' I said to Mike now. 'Unfortunate choice of words, love.' And Tyler's groan when he got it was heart-ening too.

But telling our own son to try not to worry about things he couldn't control was one thing – stopping our house guest from controlling her own destiny was quite another.

Be prepared! Was that the motto of the Scouts or the Girl Guides? Either way, it was my go-to state every morning these days. It's an actual state too; a clenching feeling in the gut that something bad is going to happen, which made me anxious, which I didn't like at all. But with Harley in the house – or not, as the case may be – perpetual high alert (hyper-vigilance, I think they call it) was a necessity as I never knew what the day would bring.

I was right to feel that way too, because today was no different. She'd barely been home for twelve hours after the second no-show by her mother when we heard the front door bang and she was gone.

It was Saturday now and I was in the kitchen, making breakfast, Mike and Tyler reading the papers at the dining-room table and having independently interpreted the sound for what it might have been, we all converged in the hall at the same time.

'Did you hear that?' I asked. 'Was that Harley going out?' I pulled the front door open and looked out onto the empty road out front. She must have moved fast because there was already no sign of her.

'Shall I go after her, Mum?' Tyler said, already bending down to pick up his trainers. 'Because I bet the police are sick of this, don't you?'

'The bloody police can get in line!' Mike said, turning back to the living room and throwing his paper onto the sofa, 'because they're not the only ones. No, Ty, you're not going after her. You're just going to carry on doing what you're doing, as will Mum, who will sit with us and have her coffee and bacon sandwich, and we will have at least *some* time to enjoy a semblance of normality in this house.' He looked at me pointedly. 'Casey, *please*, love.'

I groaned inwardly. In my head, I was already putting my shoes on. The impulse to go after her was strong. 'I don't know …' I began.

'*Leave* her,' Mike said, a little more strongly than usual.

'Dad's right, Mum,' Tyler chipped in. 'We all know what she's up to. She knows we're down here, relaxing. She could probably smell the bacon. She just wants to cause maximum anxiety for us.'

I was upset to hear Tyler talking like that. It wasn't like him at all, he was normally so empathetic. But I knew he was only saying what Mike was clearly thinking. And not a million miles away from thoughts I'd been having myself. Thoughts I'd pushed away, but still lurked there nonetheless. Even so, I felt I had to fight her corner. 'We can't think like that, sweetie,' I said. 'She's clearly disturbed, and ...'

'I'm bloody disturbed too!' Mike said, his anger now transparent. 'I mean, come on, Case, every single hospital, every single doctor. They all say the same thing – that there's nothing wrong with her, *nothing*! And I might not have any idea what they mean by "environmental", but it's certainly not this bloody environment because here, we bend over backwards for her all the *time*.'

I was shocked to see both my husband and son so angry and upset. I'd clearly failed to realise that we were not on the same page about Harley. But my gut instinct was to go, and I generally listened to it. We'd made progress when I'd last followed her and confronted her, and however scant it was (and I knew I mustn't delude myself on that score), if I could catch up with her and speak to her, I knew I would have the opportunity to reinforce whatever message I'd got across.

'Look,' I said, wiping my hands on the tea towel I was holding, 'I know you're both annoyed and I am too, but this time – I'm sorry – I'm doing it my way. I'm off to get her before she gets too far, and if I can't find her quickly, I'll be straight back, I promise. I just think she needs to know that I'm not going to passively stand by and let her do this. Please, I *need* to do this, okay?'

'I thought you said you already made that clear last time,' Mike pointed out, 'and it clearly didn't do much good, did it?'

'Reinforcement,' I said as I grabbed my jacket and my car keys. 'Please, I have to try. Mind the bacon.'

Happily, neither Mike nor Tyler tried to stop me – I think they both realised resistance was going to be futile – and within moments I was in the car and driving down the road I thought most likely that she'd have headed down. I could have been wrong of course, but, happily, my hunch had been right: I spotted her marching down the pavement on the road that led to the local park. She was just veering off down the footpath that ran down the side of it when I pulled up and jumped out of the car.

'Harley!' I yelled. 'What the hell do you think you're playing at?'

She turned and stared at me, shocked. She'd obviously thought, given that we were busy having breakfast, I wouldn't bother, which pleased me in itself.

As did the fact that she made no move to walk away from me.

'Go on,' I said. 'I'd like an explanation, please.'

She lifted her head, bobbed her chin up. 'What d'you mean, explanation? I can go for a walk if I want to, can't I?'

'No, you can't,' I said, '*actually*. Because you don't go for "walks". You go off on attention-seeking escapades is what you do.' There, I'd said it. 'Causing all kinds of upset, leaving me on pins wondering what you're up to and causing the emergency services no end of trouble when they have more than enough work on their shoulders already, as you well know. *That's* what you do!'

If she'd looked shocked before she looked truly stunned now. And not without good reason, because it was a pretty hard-hitting thing to say to her. Not to mention high-risk, because I was as good as challenging her to put up or shut up. The consequences of which were unthinkable.

She lowered her head. '*God!* I was just going for a *walk*,' she repeated, kicking at the gravel on the path with her foot.

'Harley, did anything I said to you the other day sink in?'

She rolled her eyes. '*What*?'

'*What*? That's not good enough, young lady. As in the fact that I made it clear to you that this isn't acceptable. That I'm not having you coming and going from my house anytime you please. I'm not having you put me and my family in this constant state of anxiety. You live under *my* roof, and I don't care what you might have been told by Tessa or anyone else, I'm not having you swan off whenever the fancy takes you without letting me know where you're going or when you'll be back. You might think nobody cares about you but I bloody do! So here's today's choice – you either come home, or I'm coming on your walk *with* you.'

'God's *sake*,' she said. 'Why can't you just *leave me alone*?'

I shook my head. 'Not an option.'

'*Why*? I didn't *ask* to come here.'

'You had another plan then, did you?'

'Yes! I – *God*, why can't you just leave me *alone*?'

'Because I have promised I will *look after you*, however hard you try to make it. Because—'

'So don't then! Call Tessa and tell her you're done with me! Tell her *I'm* done, because no one ever seems to listen to me. I'm *done*, *okay*? I don't want to be alive in this shitty world anymore!'

There were tears in her eyes now and every fibre of my being was screaming out to me to hug her. But I held back – I was too scared she'd recoil.

'I know,' I said instead. 'Because you've made that crystal clear, believe me. But here we are. Here *you* are. Still here. Still in pain. Still wanting to die. Yet you're not dead. Have you thought about why that might be, Harley? Even for a second? Because I'll tell you what I think. You don't want to die. You can't see a reason to live – and I get that, because you're right, your life has been shitty – but you don't want to die either. You want *help*.' Tears were rolling down her face now; good tears was my instinct. So I pressed on. 'You don't know how to ask for it. You might not even think you want it. But you're asking for it, *screaming* for it, every minute of every day; every time you cut yourself, every time you threaten to end it all and don't go through with it, every time you leave the house without telling us where you're going … Harley, if you really wanted me to leave you alone, you'd *tell* me you were going, don't you see that? You'd tell me where you were going, and when you were coming back, then you'd go somewhere else entirely, and – pff! – you'd be gone, and there'd be nothing I could do, and I would have to live with that knowledge, that loss, for ever. But you don't do that, do you? Because you don't want to die, you want *help*.'

Harley glared at me, brushed the tears from her eyes and cheeks, and glared again. 'What do *you* know?' she yelled, pushing past me.

Then to my astonishment, she walked back into the street, to my car, yanked on the passenger door handle, opened the door and climbed in.

It was my turn to be stunned now and I followed her in silence. I belted up, started the engine, met her eyes in the rear-view mirror. Opened my mouth to speak. To say something reassuring. Comforting.

She was having none of it.

'Don't,' she said. 'Just don't.'

Chapter 14

It was my birthday the following day and I didn't want any kind of fuss. Had insisted that there *be* no kind of fuss, either. It just felt all wrong to have any kind of celebration at the moment. Not with Harley still with us and everything that was going on. It seemed to me that it would only be asking for trouble. Besides, it wasn't as if it was a big birthday or anything, just my fifty-fourth and we could just as easily celebrate it another day.

But Mike was having none of it. 'We are going to celebrate your birthday and that's the end of it. I've already spoken to Riley' – had he now? – 'and we have come up with a cunning plan.'

'As in?'

He grinned mischievously. 'As in we're going round to her house. Steaks on the barbecue, and lots and lots of cake.'

'Mike, you know we can't do that. I can't leave Harley on her own here. And I doubt there's a cat's chance in hell that she'd come with us.'

An even lower chance that that, I thought. There was zero chance, obviously. And there was no way I'd countenance having the family round to me. After the conversation I'd had with Harley it just felt too much like tempting fate. Especially as when we'd returned she'd immediately gone back up to her room and no attempt by me to talk some more to her – I'd knocked and tried three times in total – got more than a 'Just please leave me alone' in reply.

'We're going,' Mike said, 'and that's an end to it.' He then proceeded to tell me that while I'd been out bringing in the washing, he'd spoken to Christine Bolton and persuaded her to come round and babysit Harley for a few hours.

'You *what*?' I squeaked. 'I can't believe you did that. On a Sunday? We can't expect her to come round here and look after Harley on a Sunday! It's her day off!'

'Believe it, because I did. And she was happy to do so. For one thing, she's on call anyway, so might just as well be here for a bit as anywhere, and for another, she agreed that you need a break – badly. Honestly, you should listen to yourself – worrying about Christine's day off? It wasn't so long ago that you had cast everyone in social services, her very much included, into the hinterland of your strong disapproval!'

Which was a very grand thing to say, especially for my husband, who wasn't usually that poetic. 'God, you didn't tell her that, did you?'

'Oh, for goodness' sake, Case – as if. I just pointed out that you were under a great deal of strain. Seriously, she honestly didn't need any persuading whatsoever. She was happy to help. And it's not like she's got to do anything, is it? Chances are, she won't even see her.'

'Unless she does another runner.'

'And if she does, I'm sure Christine will be able to handle it. She's as perfectly capable of phoning the police and EDT as we are. And sending herself an email to update herself while she's at it. So we are going to Riley's to celebrate your birthday. And that's *it*.'

The next morning, however, I was beginning to have second thoughts. Would I really enjoy myself knowing Harley was at home and that I wasn't around if she absconded? Or had a crisis like she'd had when she'd stabbed herself with that compass? I made the mistake of confiding in Mike as I sat in bed drinking my first birthday coffee.

'You know what you've got,' he said, 'a messiah complex, that's what. Whatever happens – which it might or might not – Christine can handle it. Now get your head into gear. We have a party to get to. Put her out of your mind, love. Let someone else take the mental strain for a change.'

So it was that an hour later, me, Mike and Tyler were en route to Riley's and Christine's reassuring presence had indeed set my mind at rest. While at the same time furiously wondering about the enormous bag in the back of the car which apparently contained Mike's surprise present for me.

So it was the first thing I wanted to open when we fetched up at Riley's and where, contrary to my orders, a massive fuss did seem to have been made. Because the day was so warm, they'd hung bunting and balloons all round their garden, plus fixed a huge banner-like appendage to the back of one of the garden chairs, which had 'Twenty-One Today!' emblazoned across it in cut-out foil letters.

I could have wept, but was far too excited. Not least, noting the weight of the wrapping-paper-covered box Mike now placed in front of me.

'Go on, Nanna,' Levi urged. 'It might be a PlayStation!'

'It's way too big for a PlayStation,' his brother Jackson observed. 'Maybe it's one of those fold-up bikes for old people,' he added, ducking before I could cuff him round the ear.

It was neither. It was something I had wanted for ages. A beautiful Victorian tea set, in a pretty wildflower pattern, complete with two three-tiered cake stands and the *pièce de résistance*, not just a teapot, but also a matching coffee jug.

Mike rolled his eyes. 'Well, *obviously*.'

'It's beautiful,' I said, carefully inspecting one of the bone-china cups. 'And so elegant. So *posh*. Ooh, I can't wait to have a posh tea party so I can show it off! Which, by the way,' I cast my gaze around at my oh-so precious family, 'means none of you common lot will be invited.

But how did you know?' I asked Mike, genuinely aghast that he'd been so thoughtful.

He laughed. 'Ah, I don't know, let me see ... *Oh, babes,*' he said, putting on a high-pitched voice and flapping his arms about, '*look at that on the telly! Oh, I'd love some proper old-fashioned tea-party china. Oh, Mike, did I tell you that Lauren's mum has a beautiful china tea set, all of it matching?*'

'Oh, shut up!' I laughed, recalling some of the less subtle hints I'd made. They'd been over the years, mind, not recent, so I had waited a while. Anyway, I had it now and it was better than any of the others I'd envied because mine had a coffee pot too.

And a whole load of other lovely presents besides. New perfume, a load of smellies and some razzy multicoloured socks from Tyler – six pairs in all and not a matching pair between them. 'Save you work, they will, Mum,' he explained once I'd opened them. 'No sorting, you can put any one with any other one. Simples!'

There was also a lavender-filled microwaveable hot-water bottle, in the shape of a teddy bear from Kieron and Lauren. 'That's to keep you warm in the middle of the night,' Kieron explained, 'when you're round at ours sleeping on the sofa.'

'Win win, then,' I said, feeling tearful. Because it was.

But as I sat among my loved ones and privately acknowledged that Mike had been right – it was *so* good to be celebrating with them all today – I couldn't help but think of Harley, back at home. When was the last time anyone had bought her a present? It was obviously on the file, but with the days of our twenty-eight days together whizzing by so stressfully and eventfully, I realised I hadn't even thought to find out when her birthday was. Another sad fact of a sad situation.

A sad situation which was destined to become sadder. Lovely as the day was it was always going to be tempered with melancholy and I felt my mood plunge the minute Mike's key was in the door.

'Everything okay here?' I asked Christine, who'd come into the hall to greet us.

'All quiet,' she said. 'I popped up a couple of times to check on her, but she didn't want to talk to me. And I obviously didn't push it, knowing how things are. I just went up ten minutes' back. I think she's listening to music. So all well. And you've had a lovely time, yes?'

I nodded. 'Brought back a lot of cake too. I thought you might like to take a hunk back for you and your husband. Would you?'

'Would I? Ahem – is the Pope Catholic?'

Which was why we had our backs turned when Tyler came into the kitchen. He'd gone upstairs to use the bathroom because Mike had beaten him to the loo downstairs and now, moments later, he was back down.

'Mum,' he said. We both turned. His face told a story. And not a jolly one.

'What's up, love?' I asked, feeling fear clutch at my insides.

'I think you need to come upstairs and see the bathroom.'

'Oh, God!' I said. 'Harley?'

He shook his head. 'She's not in there.'

'She's in her room,' Christine said. 'I know she is.' I could hear the panic in her voice. 'She couldn't have got past me, I was up there literally ten minutes' ago.'

Tyler beckoned. 'She's in her room. I can hear her. Come on. Come up and see.'

We trooped up behind him to the bathroom and followed him in. To what looked like the aftermath of a small massacre. Blood. On the floor tiles, on the wall tiles, on the sink and the bath sides. 'What the—?' Christine didn't even bother finishing what she was saying. We were all speechless. Tyler's face was grey.

'What's she been doing, Mum?' he eventually whispered. 'Has she been cutting herself?'

And then some, I thought, and then some. And what sort of state, given all this, might she be in right this minute?

I went straight across the landing to her bedroom and didn't knock, just went straight in.

And there was Harley, earbuds in, sitting on her bed, propped by pillows, knees up, quietly scrolling through her mobile. The only evidence of what she'd done was peeking out from the sleeves of her long-sleeved T-shirt in the form of whatever she'd found to use to bandage her wrists. Actual bandages, I could see – presumably from my bathroom cabinet.

Let Me Go

It was all just too much – what she'd done, and what she'd left in the bathroom. I didn't know where to start – what to say to her.

Tyler did. 'What the *hell* have you been doing in our bathroom?' he demanded.

One at a time, she pulled the earbuds from her ears. 'Wha–? Look, sorry, okay? I didn't know you'd be back so soon, did I?' Then, in an almost leisurely fashion, she swung her legs around and put her feet down on the floor. 'Look, sorry, okay?' she said to me as she stood up. 'I'll clear it up now.'

If I hadn't known what to say before I certainly didn't now. Neither did Christine. And now Tyler just gaped at me. 'Is she for *real*?' he hissed as we stood aside to let her pass us.

'Come on,' I said, 'let's just all go back downstairs.'

Chapter 15

That night, perhaps as a consequence of the whole birthday debacle, Harley gave us the slip in the small hours. The first I knew of it was when my mobile rang at seven the following morning and it was the police, telling me she was currently with them.

We'd not known a thing about it, and perhaps that was a blessing, because if I had, I would have suffered agonies of guilt and mortification. I didn't know if she was punishing us, but that was certainly possible because after Christine had left, shaken ('I genuinely never heard a thing, honestly!'), Mike hadn't been able to stop himself losing it with her. He'd gone up there – she was still cleaning the bathroom at the time – and had given her both barrels.

I couldn't have stopped him if I'd wanted to, though only half of me did. It wasn't so much the self-harming (no one's heart could fail to bleed about that). It was the fact that she'd left the mess – a mess that she must have made deliberately – for any of us, including Tyler, to find. It was almost as if that had been her intention. So, a cry for help, definitely. But it wouldn't be coming from one quarter.

'I draw the line, Case,' he'd said grimly, 'when it comes to my children. My sympathy can stretch so far – it stretches more than most, believe me – but I will *not* have her treat us like this. You've tried *so* hard and this is how she repays you. Well, I'm sorry, but I cannot *wait* for this week to be up! And I'm sorry if it was wrong, but I told her that too. We've got to protect our own.'

And so she'd gone again.

But was now apparently back. Or at least wanting to come back. They'd picked her up at dawn, after having been flagged down in their patrol car by a homeless man – one of two with which she'd apparently spent the remainder of the night, sleeping rough under a tree in a local park.

'She's fine,' the constable told me. 'They were just happy to hand her over to us, as you can imagine, since she refused to tell them anything about what she was doing there, or what her name was, or where she lived, and they were obviously terrified at the prospect of taking responsibility for her – not to mention worrying about being arrested. So all's well that ends well. And now she's admitted who she is and where she's billeted, we'll bring her back now, if that's okay with you?'

All of which made for an uncomfortable encounter when they appeared half an hour later, since they questioned me at length about the circumstances of her giving me the slip which, since I'd never met them before, and they were oblivious to the circumstances, must have made them see me as a pretty careless foster carer.

I stammered my way through a lame explanation, about how she hardly ever left her room and that was, for her, normal behaviour, but I could tell they were far from convinced.

And perhaps I had been careless – or, perhaps worse, totally misguided – because that same afternoon, after, understandably, sleeping all morning, Harley appeared in the kitchen, dressed, and with her jacket on, while I was in the middle of putting my online grocery shop away. (I didn't much like online grocery shopping but needs must.) She looked as calm and self-possessed as I think I'd ever seen her.

'I'm going for a walk,' she said. 'To the park, for an hour. I'll see you later.' Then turned around, left the kitchen and went out into the hall. A second later, I heard the front door close behind her.

Were it capable of doing so, my blood would have run cold. As it was I just stood there, a tin of beans in each hand, and thought, 'Oh, *no*.'

'Harley, wait!' I called out, once I'd recovered my wits. 'Please,' I added, running into the hall. I opened the door. She was just in sight but would soon be gone, round the corner. And Ty had taken my car to work. Oh, *no*.

Let Me Go

And all I had on my feet was a pair of socks. Glancing back into the hall in the faint hope that I'd left my trainers on the stairs – not that they would be because I'd spent the morning tidying up – I realised if I were to give chase, then it would be practically barefoot. Well, if it was good enough for Zola Budd, it was good enough for me.

'Harley!' I yelled manically as I ran after her. 'Harley, wait!' But as soon as I said that, my foot landed on something sharp and painful enough to make me howl. There was no way I could hobble after her like this.

There was therefore no choice. Dejected and very annoyed, I instead hobbled back to the house and up to her room, dialling 999 on my mobile as I went. As had been the case before, as per instructions, I could just wait for her to return, and perhaps should, but I knew better. I knew what I'd said to her that day in the park. That if she really wanted to die she'd have played things very differently. She wouldn't sneak out of the house while our backs were turned or we were sleeping. She'd come right up to me *and tell me she was going for a walk*. 'To the park for an hour,' she'd said. 'I'll see you later.' She had *played* me.

And yet – and there was no time to think about why – a search of her room while I was waiting to be transferred to the right person revealed that she had left me a gift.

It was a piece of paper from the same exercise book she'd written the last note on and she'd left it beneath her pillow. A note. A suicide note.

So on the one hand she'd told me something to mis-direct me and here, in complete contrast, was at least half a clue as to where she was really intent on going. Or was it a double-bluff? No, I thought. No. Perhaps it was a test – even if she hadn't consciously meant to offer it. I'd only find this if I tried hard enough. If I *cared* enough to look. And if I didn't that would be proof positive that she really had no reason to go on living, since it would confirm the world really *didn't* care.

Or perhaps she'd just written it then abandoned it.

Either way, I was sitting on Harley's bed with the note in my hand by the time I'd cleared the first hurdle of the name, rank and serial number identification process and could finally explain fully to the police what I was calling about. 'I have the note right here,' I told the dispatcher. 'And it's unquestionably a suicide note.'

The officer asked me to read it out to him.

Please, please don't come looking for me, Casey. You'll be too late anyway. I've already checked the train times from … Please, just let me go. I have had it with this life and I don't want to live. Tell my mum and my sister I'm sorry, and that I don't blame them. I apologise. It's not your fault. Harley.

Of course, I then had to go through the usual longer list of questions, the whole physical description thing, my impressions about her mental state and any ideas I might have had about where she'd head for. Which was when I realised she'd left me another gift as well. Her laptop, which was open on the chest of drawers opposite, with several tabs open, the top of which was Google Maps. I leapt up and went to it. I knew exactly what I was seeing. 'The road bridge before the nearest station from here,' I told them hurriedly. 'It has to be that one. I have the map right in front of me.' I did my best to explain where I meant. 'It has to be – she's on foot and I don't think she has any money.'

And thankfully – *so* thankfully – because of the existence of the note, the woman told me that a squad car had already been dispatched. She would now radio everything through to the attending officers and hopefully they'd be able to track her down.

This calmed me a little and once I'd disconnected the call, I read the note again, trying to see between the lines. I kept telling myself that if someone genuinely wanted to kill themselves, they would be unlikely to leave such an obvious clue. And they definitely wouldn't leave their laptop open. So she *wanted* me to track her down – she must do.

And I was right. Only minutes later, my phone rang. 'We have Harley in our car, Mrs Watson,' an officer told me. 'She's absolutely fine, just a bit shaken up and teary, but she has asked us to bring her back to you. Is that alright?'

More food for thought as my racing heart stopped racing. Because this was the first time Harley had actually asked to come back home to us; not demanded to be detained under the Mental Health Act, in order that she be taken to a hospital, or made to come back by whichever police officers had found her. Did this constitute progress in some tiny way? I wasn't sure, but I was sure as hell going to take it as such.

'Yes, of course,' I said immediately.

I hung up, went into the kitchen and started putting the rest of the shopping away. And then, strangely, the same police officer called again. 'Just fuelling up,' he said, 'and while we're here, I thought I'd call you while Harley's in the car with my colleague. Just to let you know that when we found her, she wasn't on the bridge. She was sitting in a bus shelter just down the road a little ways. Just sitting there, on the bench, scrolling through her phone. I don't know if that's of any use to you, but I thought you should know.'

'It's of great use,' I assured him.

So my second action when she was delivered back fifteen minutes later (the first obviously being to thank the police officers) was to make her sit down at the kitchen table and pass her the note.

My first instinct was to point to where she'd mentioned having already checked the train times and ask her why she'd done that if she didn't want me to go after her. And to ask her why she'd left her laptop open. But since she'd handed my own words back to me only less than an hour earlier, I was naturally reluctant to bring that to her attention in case next time she left us, be it with or without us knowing, she noted that the best way to ensure I wouldn't have a clue where she was going would be to slip away *without* leaving clues.

'You know, Harley,' I said gently – she was still quietly crying – 'we don't have very many days left together now, do we?' She shook her head. 'Which means there's very little time left for me to try and help you.' I nodded towards the note. 'And this tells me you do want me to help you. So, please, love, let me. Sit with me. Sit here and cry with me if that's what you need to do. Just, please, don't go back up to that room and be all on your own. Stay down here with me for a bit. We don't need to talk if you don't want to. Just try to believe that I'm here for you. That I can help you.'

She looked at me then. Shook her head and wiped tears from her cheeks. 'But you can't,' she said. 'I know you want to, but you can't. No one can.'

Then she pushed her chair back, stood up and left the kitchen.

And though I attempted some further dialogue through her bedroom door a couple of times more, she had absolutely nothing else to say to me.

The rest of the day continued much like any other. I had dutifully deposited a sandwich and drink for her (somewhat late) lunch, then spent the afternoon writing up a report on the day's events, trying to put into words what I was struggling to put into any kind of order in my brain. If this was a game – make a plan that includes careful provision for it to be thwarted, come home, say nothing, do nothing, go to bed, repeat – then I was a complete loss to know how to play it. What curveballs could I realistically lob into the game with my time on the playing field almost up? Any? So would she leave us as she'd come to us? Still alive? Still an enigma? I think my spirit then was at its lowest ebb.

At least Tyler seemed in better spirits when he came home from his shift. He'd said nothing more about the bloodbath in the bathroom and I hadn't either, and I obviously wasn't going to mention today's dramas.

'You okay, sweetie?' I asked him when he came down for his tea after changing. 'I mean okay as in okay-okay? Nothing you want to get off your chest?'

He came straight across and hugged me. 'I'm fine,' he said. 'Are *you* fine? You don't look it.'

I'd made his favourite for tea as he was off out football training. 'Just tired out from slaving away at a hot stove,' I told him. 'Lasagne and salad,' I said as I set down his plate at the table. 'Made just the way you like it, sir.'

Tyler gave it the once-over, then grinned and shook his head. 'Not quite, Mother dearest. No chips? No garlic bread? Correct me if I'm wrong, but there was only you on The Eternal Diet in this house last time I checked, so why must the rest of us suffer?'

So he *was* fine. 'Eat, boy,' I said, 'and stop complaining. Healthy is as healthy does and I'm trying to retrain your brain. If you must, you can go and get some bread from the kitchen but—'

At which point, my mobile butted in. It was Kieron, in a bit of a state.

'Mum, Mum, something's wrong! I'm at the hospital with Lauren – you need to get here, *now*.'

My heart sank immediately at the tone of his voice. It could be nothing – Lauren was booked in for a C-section in three weeks' time – but on the other hand ... 'Calm down, Kieron,' I said firmly. '*Breathe*, okay? Deep slow breaths. So, tell me. What's wrong, sweetie? Is it the baby?'

'She's gone into early labour, Mum.' Kieron was almost crying at this point, I could tell. 'They say they're going to try to stop it, but they can't be sure they can. She's having contractions, like, every five minutes – that can't be right, can it? It's too *early*. It might be dangerous, mightn't it? Can you get here, Mum, please? Like, as in *now*?'

I glanced at the clock and assured him I would get there as fast as I could. But it would be at least twenty minutes before Mike got home and then another twenty-minute drive to the hospital and I didn't want to leave Ty home alone with Harley. The only trouble was that neither did I want to leave it that long to be with my other son, who would, I knew, become increasingly distraught. And who was currently in no state to be lectured to about breathing. The only thing that would calm him down, I knew, would be my physically being there.

'Just go, Mum!' Tyler said after I filled him in on what was happening. 'Look, stop worrying. You said yourself that if she wants to go, we have to let her. And if she does, then I'll call Dad, and EDT, and whoever. Just go! Honestly, I swear it'll be fine.'

'Show me where the numbers are, Ty,' I said. 'Come on, for EDT and for Christine, just so I know. I need to know that you know.'

'Top of the fridge, Mother. Front page of your pink book. Now *go!*'

'Promise me you'll get Dad to ring me the minute he gets back,' I said as I left the house, trying to calm myself down. The truth is, all thoughts of Harley and what she may or may not do were pushed firmly to the back of my mind by that point anyway. I simply couldn't worry about her right now and instead needed to focus on my own family and what they were facing.

And as I rushed onto the maternity unit and saw Kieron's anxious face, I knew I had done the right thing. He was pacing the corridor, waiting for me, massively over-breathing – well on his way to a full-blown panic attack, in fact. Without me there, he'd be no use to poor Lauren. I wrapped him up in a reassuring hug.

'They can't stop it, Mum,' he sniffed, once I'd calmed him down enough to get some sense from him. 'The baby is coming. They say it's not too early, and that everything should be okay, but Lauren is so scared, Mum, and I don't know how to help her. Her mum and dad are trying to get here, but that's going to be hours yet! What if everything *isn't* okay?'

Let Me Go

Having been present at so many family births, a familiar instinct immediately kicked in. I was no longer on high alert – the marked lack of any kind of panic from the staff made it plain they weren't worried – and as the calmness flowed over me I physically pushed up my cardigan sleeves, smiled and stroked my son's arm, and went into the labour room with him to see to Lauren.

Of the two of them, Lauren is always the calm one. But she was also in labour almost a month before her due date and I could see the anxiety writ large on her pink and sheeny face, especially as she'd been down for a caesarean. But they were apparently unruffled because the baby was so early. Being so much smaller than expected, had it waited till term, they seemed happy that all would be well. I smoothed her hair back. 'Everything is going to be just fine, silly,' I told her. 'This is nature being nature, just taking its course. And I'm going to be here every step of the way now, so you just try to relax, sweetie, and go with it.'

Lauren grabbed hold of the gas-and-air mixture she'd been using and started sucking in the painkilling concoction. 'Am I? Is the baby going to be fine?' she rasped before another huge contraction took over.

I grabbed Kieron's hand and firmly guided it to Lauren's so she could squeeze the life out of his rather than mine. 'Absolutely!' I said. 'Now just breathe, use your gas and air, and try to get some rest in between the pains.'

There was no other choice really. When a baby decides to push its way into the world, it cares not a jot that a different date was marked on the calendar. And that's exactly what baby Carter had obviously planned on doing and, indeed, did, some five hours later. He was a beautiful boy and it was wonderful to be there and have the privilege of holding him while Kieron gave Lauren – the pair of them in floods of tears – a much-needed congratulatory hug.

It was almost 1 a.m. by the time I was finally able to pull my phone out and tell Mike and Ty that the newest member of the Watson clan had arrived safely, at which point I saw Mike had been trying to contact *me*. Not a call – so it clearly wasn't anything super-urgent. Just a trio of texts, two a couple of hours back, the last only fifteen minutes previously, telling me not to worry, but asking me to call him whenever I had a chance.

Knowing he was probably awake still, I walked out of the ward and a little way down the hospital corridor to call him.

'It's a little boy,' I announced, feeling a bit weepy myself at that point. 'They're calling him Carter and everything is okay. You alright? I've just seen your messages.'

'Well, I am now,' Mike said, the emphasis very much on the 'now' part. 'But bloody Harley ran away again earlier. I thought all was quiet up there, but she walked down around 7 p.m. and was straight out the door. I tried to stop her, but other than grabbing her and holding on to her, there was little else I could do.'

'Oh *God*,' I said, a familiar heaviness settling over and smothering my grandmotherly elation. 'Is she back now, then? Did she leave a note again? What's she said?'

'That's why I needed to talk to you. Yes, the police found her but only in the last hour. Apparently she was on top of the bridge over the bypass, threatening to jump, and, well, turns out you're going to see her before I do.'

Mike went on to explain that Harley had gone back to throwing in her 'detain me for my own safety' speech and as there were no available beds at any local psychiatric hospitals, she was currently, as in right now, in transit to another – the district general, the very hospital I was at.

'She's being taken to the children's ward,' Mike explained, 'and kept under the supervision of a police officer – she might well be there already, actually – and they'll stay only till either you go and take over from them, or—'

'Take over from them? Why?'

'He said it was because she might be a danger to herself or the other children, or abscond again – that was the gist of it. Because that hospital is just a normal hospital and not geared up for patients with mental health issues. They need someone to stay with her until someone from the CAMHS crisis team shows up.'

'Well, that's not bloody likely,' I said in response. 'At least not until office hours in the morning.'

'Well, look,' Mike said, 'I've explained to the police the situation you're in right now and they do understand,

and you have every right to just come home when you can. They're not demanding that you step in to relieve them or anything. It's just their job to ask, I suppose, but I'll leave it up to you. Either way, love, I have to get to bed pretty soon, otherwise I'll be fit for nothing at work tomorrow.'

I looked down the corridor in one direction – the children's ward was two corridors away from where I stood – then I looked in the other. The way I had come. Of course I'd stay. Clear as it was that I had struggled to connect with Harley, that I'd had nothing to contribute, this I *could* do. And who knew? Perhaps just the act of my staying with her – that act of being there for her – would be enough evidence to convince her that I *did* care. That I cared that she somehow found a reason to live. If it meant sitting there all night then so be it.

But not quite yet, because I knew she was safe. And I had a tiny new family member to welcome, to cuddle. A precious moment for giving thanks, for counting blessings, for bonding. *Then* I'd go to her. The police officer could wait for a bit longer. Another half an hour wouldn't hurt.

Chapter 16

It was around 2 a.m. when I finally got ushered into the children's ward, which was lit only by the faintest of lights. I was embarrassed to find a tired-looking security guard stationed outside the ward, yawning, and then to be told by the nurse, who didn't look tired, just inconvenienced, all the same things that Mike had already told me. I thanked her. So many people, put to so much inconvenience and worry. I knew it was silly, and I knew I was overly emotional, but I still felt responsible. I couldn't help it.

It was quite spooky tiptoeing around a hospital during the early hours, and more so on this ward full of slumbering little ones. Apart from the occasional bleep of some piece of equipment, and the low tones of soft snores and snuffles, it was really quiet. I was led past cots with poorly babies in, beds bearing sleeping toddlers, and then on to the very end of the ward, which was where it seemed they housed the older kids.

Thankfully, Harley had been put in an area slightly apart – not quite a side room but sufficiently far away from the nearest patients that we could talk, even if it had to be in whispers. There was a curtain around her bed and two police officers sitting on either side of it – one was male, and one was female, and both looked completely exhausted. I wondered what time they had started their shifts; that they'd long passed clocking-off time seemed all too evident by the way they drooped in their chairs.

They sat up straight when we appeared round the curtain, but Harley – wide awake and staring up towards the ceiling – didn't even turn her head to look my way. 'You okay, sweetie?' I asked anyway, before introducing myself to the officers – perhaps she genuinely hadn't heard us arrive and was far away, lost in her thoughts. Either way, she said nothing in reply to me.

'I'm sorry it's taken so long,' I said. 'But my daughter-in-law was rushed in earlier, in labour, so it's been quite a night already, not to mention a long one,' I added with a smile.

The female officer stood up and smiled. 'New baby, then? Congratulations.'

'A little boy, yes, and thank you. He's just gorgeous.'

The other officer stood up too – they were clearly keen to get away now. 'Yes, congratulations,' he added. 'Quite a night for you, indeed.' He turned to Harley, as if to illustrate, and that was when I noticed the angry-looking wounds around her neck.

Let Me Go

Oh, no. I thought. *Again.* 'Oh, love!' I said, perching on the side of the bed. 'What did you do?'

In answer, she turned away from me and tugged the sheet up to cover her entire head. She clearly had no intention of speaking to me. The male officer then gestured that we all step away from the bed for a moment, so he and his colleague could fill me in instead.

'Seems she used some kind of ligature,' he explained, 'to tie herself to a tree branch, and had passed out, the witness thinks, before it came undone.'

My heart would have skipped a beat if it hadn't already been racing – I'd drunk an awful lot of coffee since I'd got there. 'She tried to hang herself?'

He nodded. 'Lucky girl that there was someone passing by. He tried to help her, but as soon as she'd properly regained consciousness, she took off. Fortunately he had the presence of mind to go after her, calling 999 as he did so. And though he lost her, he was pretty sure he knew where she was headed – to the bridge over the bypass. She wouldn't be the first drawn to that spot, would she?' he added, frowning.

So this time she hadn't gone to the railway. Had she been googling the area again? Because he was right. Almost every large town or city has its infamous suicide spot. That was ours. I thought again, then, about the horrors of the internet; of such gruesome information being shared.

'Anyway, we've—' the female officer began, but before she could get anything else out, she was drowned out by

Harley's voice. 'I am *here*,' she barked, causing a nurse to scurry back to us to admonish her about the noise.

We returned to her bedside, where she had now thrown the sheet back and sat up. 'And if you don't mind,' she added, pointing a finger in my direction, 'I'd like her to go, please.' She then turned to me. 'Don't worry, I'm sure they'll bring me back to you tomorrow.' Then she lay back again and turned on her side facing away from me.

I was gobsmacked. She'd spoken to me in some pretty snappy ways, but she'd never spoken to me quite like that before. 'Harley, love,' I started, feeling stung by *what* she'd said as well. What the hell had I done? As in specifically. Right now. That I hadn't done before? Of course. Been called away, to attend to my own family. A new, much-anticipated baby. Had put their needs ahead of hers again, just as had happened on my birthday. Had that got to her? Sad though the thought was, it also suggested something positive. That she did seem to care that I cared.

More than that, though, I was struck by the realisation that she had, this time, while I was off looking after my own kids, made another, much more serious, attempt to end her life. Did she not want me there now because she was sick of me trying to talk to her about it, or because she'd decided she could more easily give the police officers the slip if I left, so she could try again? It seemed an odd choice to make, if that was her reasoning, and I was too tired to try and work it out, to second-guess her.

If I sat in one of the chairs, I knew I'd fall asleep in seconds, not least because I was probably old enough to be either of the officers' mothers. And right now, my age was definitely catching up with me.

'Please,' she said from beneath the covers, 'just leave me *alone*.'

Which left us all at a bit of an impasse. 'I'm so sorry about this,' I said to the officers, once we'd retreated back to the other side of the curtain, 'but she clearly doesn't want me here. Is there any news from EDT?' I knew the law was clear: given her situation she needed twenty-four-hour supervision, so if I didn't stay, and no one from EDT could be spared to take over, then they would have no choice – well, at least one of them wouldn't – but to stay with her overnight instead. Which made me feel terrible.

But the female officer smiled in understanding. 'No, but don't worry,' she said. 'I'm sure someone will turn up eventually. We'll be fine here in the meantime. Go on, you get back to your family.'

'Yes, get back to your *family*,' Harley added, from under the covers. I was clearly going to be no use here. So I did.

I really did feel pretty bad as I drove home, because I felt my place, in this scenario, was to be with Harley, especially as the baby had been delivered safely. Looking after her was my job, after all. I knew not a person in the world would castigate me for not insisting that I stay, particularly given that she was so adamant that I didn't, but it felt all wrong to leave two police officers minding a teenager in a hospital, given that we were so short of police officers and they had all sorts of better things to do – like the proverbial 'being out there and catching criminals'. Not that I was the only foster carer in this situation – far from it. Calling on the police for this kind of thing was happening more and more often simply because there wasn't another service able to step in. Government cuts had meant massive holes in social care budgets across the board and this was the kind of situation that often resulted. Police taken off the streets to act as temporary jailors, nursemaids, counsellors and a whole host of other professions they had never signed up for.

But I also felt bad about myself. Because I'd failed her. It felt as if every glimmer of connection between us – few and far between, I had to admit – had once again been proved as the mirage it clearly was. I was kidding myself if I thought I'd made any progress. I wasn't stupid – this wasn't about her trusting me, or feeling comfortable around us as a family, or listening to my various 'wisdoms', because right now I felt she was beyond making meaningful relationships – but it was about that instinctive sense that, in different circumstances, we could have forged a positive relationship, just as I'd managed to do with all kinds of troubled kids before her. It just wasn't happening this time and I was beginning to accept that perhaps it never would. Which made me sad – was I losing my touch with kids, somehow? Was it because she could sense that, despite my protestations otherwise, I was only invested in her up to a point? Because that was the truth of it, wasn't it?

I knew it was the kind of soul-searching that never went well when embarked on in the middle of the night, tired, but Harley's rejection had been very public and very clear and however much I told myself not to take it personally, I couldn't seem to help it.

I got home to a cold, silent house, a little after three. Mike and Tyler had long since gone to bed and I was so tired by now that I simply hung up my coat and bag, and quietly crept upstairs and straight into bed, trying to banish the fostering blues and ensure myself sweet dreams by concentrating on my beautiful new grandson. But somehow the fact that I had been blessed with another grandson only highlighted the gulf between Harley's life and ours, so it was a good while before I finally drifted off, chanting *tomorrow is another day* in my head, over and over.

Mike must have been uncharacteristically quiet getting ready for work – either that or I had slept like a hibernating bear – because the next morning, it was ten before I finally surfaced, and, refreshed now, and feeling at least a little more positive, I headed straight back to the hospital.

Though I didn't head for the children's ward first. Just like I needed my first two cups of coffee, I knew a shot of Carter would help set me up for the day.

It did. Though I was also a little shocked by how small he was. I'd been so preoccupied with helping to support Lauren through her labour that I'd completely forgotten that he was almost a month premature. I'd just been so delighted that he was here.

So it was great to inspect him again and be able to banish any worries. At six pounds two ounces, he was a respectable weight and when I held him, felt bonny, to boot.

'Just imagine how big he'd have been if I'd gone full term!' Lauren said as I sat with him in my arms and marvelled at his tiny hands and fingernails. 'And you know, now it's all over, I'm so glad it happened this way – because having him naturally means I'm already up and about, instead of sitting around recovering from surgery for weeks on end. They're letting me go home as soon as the doctor's been round.'

'Oh well, in that case, text me when they discharge you, love, and I'll see if I can coordinate the time with taking Harley back. If you don't mind doing a car share, of course.'

'That would probably work, actually. Save Kieron dragging all the way up here with Dee Dee. I already have my new baby seat—' she nodded to where it was stationed in the corner. 'Mum and Dad brought it with them.'

'What time did they get here?'

'Five a.m! The midwife let them in, so they could say hello to Carter, but they've gone home to catch up on sleep for a bit too, so if I could come with you, that would suit everyone perfectly. And I'd like to meet Harley finally. How's she doing?'

I'd purposely given Lauren only the very edited highlights so far. In her condition she didn't need her mind filled with sad things, after all. But now I mused on the reality of her being able to 'meet Harley' – visions of both the logistics (who'd sit where, for starters) and the contrast. Between the happiness of a new life and the despair of the suicidal. What had I been thinking, offering in the first place?

Still, I'd done it now, so there was no getting round it.

And there was no getting round facing Harley either. Not that I didn't want to see how she was doing. I was just anxious that as soon as I *did* see her, I suspected it would be clear that my hunch was right: that I was never going to get through to her.

When I arrived on the ward, however, she wasn't there.

'Are you here for Harley?' the staff nurse asked as I began making my way down to the bed in the farthest corner. 'Only she's just gone in to see the psychiatrist. I did ask her if I should I take you in when you got here, but she said no. So, unless you'd like me to ask again?'

'No, no, that's fine,' I said, feeling as resigned as my voice must have sounded. 'Should I just wait here?' I indicated the chair at the bedside. Only one now. The other must have been taken away. I wondered how long the police officers had had to stay.

'Yes, please,' the nurse said. 'Can I get you a drink of water or anything from the vending machine? You've just missed the morning trolley, I'm afraid.'

'That's kind of you,' I said, remembering the last time I'd sampled hospital coffee. 'But no, I'm fine, thank you. I'll just sit here and read on my phone, if that's okay?'

Or, rather, read all the congratulatory posts from friends on social media and share endless photos of Carter with the wider family on WhatsApp, which was such a lovely thing to lose myself in that when a shadow passed by – the same nurse, come to tell me the doctor wanted to see me – I was, at least metaphorically, miles away.

I was brought back to reality pretty sharpish though. While Harley was whisked away by another nurse, to collect her things and do whatever else needed to be done to discharge her, I had my turn in front of yet another medical professional, listening to all the reasons why they didn't consider Harley mentally ill. That she was care-seeking, manipulative and that her problems were 'environmental' and, as such, her care needed to be overseen by social services.

All well and good for them, I thought. They didn't have to live every day with the very real threat that she would successfully commit suicide. They didn't have to use at least one of the emergency services almost every day either, did they? Their whole stance seemed ridiculous, but I didn't have the energy to argue. I didn't have the expertise for a start. I mean, I wasn't a doctor, was I?

How on earth could I dispute what a professional was telling me?

I was quite thankful, at the end of it, to open up a text from Lauren saying that she was sorted out for a lift home with Carter as her parents, having power-napped, had come back to collect her.

But I was down in the dumps, too. Harley didn't say a single word to me. Not one.

All the way down the ward, out of the hospital, into the car park and into the car. Not one. So, halfway home, I lost it. Couldn't stop myself.

'You are breaking my heart, Harley. You know that? I don't know what to say to you. I don't know what to do for you. I've been doing this job for more years than you've been on this earth, I've looked after kids of every age, every background, with every problem, and I am still all out of ideas about how I can try to help you. And now I'm almost out of time too. But for what it's worth, I can promise you that however bad you feel right now, the cliché is true. Where there is life there *is* hope, even if you can't see it right now. It doesn't matter a jot whether you believe me, I just know it's true. Take Tyler. Shall I tell you just how bad his life had been when he came to us? He was eleven.' I saw a flicker of something cross her face when I said that. It was clearly a shock. 'He was just eleven and I was asked to go and fetch him from a police station, where he'd been arrested for attacking his stepmother with a kitchen knife.' Another flicker in her eyes. 'His birth mother was a heroin addict and he lived with her till he was three, when she died, at their home, of an overdose, when he was there. So they tracked his father down – a man who had never even met him – and he eventually agreed to take him on. Except it was difficult, because he had a new wife, a new life and a new baby too, and she really, really didn't want to take on Tyler. In fact, I'd probably go so far as to say she hated him. So life was pretty horrible – she was pretty horrible *to* him – and, bit by bit, he became more and more lonely, and sad, and also very angry, as you can probably imagine, because he'd lost his mother, his stepmother was cruel to him daily, and his father refused to stand up for him. Because, in truth, he didn't want him either. So when he was arrested he was also abandoned. Because they refused to have him back and he went into care.' Here, I paused. I was becoming a bit emotional now.

I cleared my throat. 'The thing is, Harley, I don't know enough about you, about your family, about your sister, about anything, to know what's going to happen to you next. But what I do know is that just as life changes for the worse, it can also change for the *better*. No matter how awful the circumstances.'

I shut up then, before I descended into dispensing homilies and clichés, and in the misguided hope that, having said my piece, I might have inspired her to reflect. That in not prodding about *her*, I might change the record. That some small sea-change might occur.

It didn't. She didn't say anything in response, and

as soon as we were back, she headed straight back up the stairs.

I honestly felt like screaming. Anything, just to get a reaction. Anything, just to create a hairline crack in that impenetrable shell.

Though in one sense, it helped my resolve. I'd failed. Made no progress with Harley since day one of the placement. And if I couldn't get close to her then it was obviously the right thing to force everyone's hands and move her on to somewhere – someone – who might do better. In an ideal world, a 'forever' family, where she could make a fresh start if her mother, as seemed so likely now, failed her.

But at the same time I knew what would be coming. A phone call, an email, a visit – perhaps all of them – suggesting that now that my grandson was safely delivered could I perhaps extend the stay beyond those twenty-eight days. I knew how their minds worked. With Carter here, they would argue, there was no urgency to move Harley on, as I no longer needed to be free for Lauren at a moment's notice. On the contrary, I argued with myself, I would probably be needed even more now. So, I knew the time had come to start gearing myself up to say the right thing, if and when that call came. The right thing for both of us.

Which was all well and good, and head-over-heart, and very sensible. But, as ever, the heart wasn't listening. And the heart told that cruel head to quieten down and think a little harder about the poor child who had no one else in her corner. No one else to help her see that life *was* worth living.

I thought fondly of Will Fisher, the lovely young man who'd been Tyler's social worker and whom Tyler was extremely close to still. In that respect, life was a lottery and I was sad that, in all the time Tessa had been working with Harley's family, a similar bond hadn't been struck. Just to know she had at least *someone* else in her corner. It was nobody's fault, it just was.

So even though the sensible head argued back and urged caution, well, I think we all know how that usually pans out. And so it did in this case.

So on what would usually have been a day of great celebration – another grandchild – instead I was deep in thought about another child. One who wasn't new to the world, far from it – had quite literally been hanging on to life by a thread. And, quite apart from my own machinations, I still couldn't get my head around the fact that nobody was willing to section her.

I was still pondering all of this, weighing up the pros and cons of an extension, when, at eight thirty that evening, Tyler off on another sleepover at Denver's, and Mike and I just settling down with a police procedural on the telly, Harley burst into the living room, waving her mobile phone in the air like a woman possessed.

'We need to phone the police, Casey, now!' she yelled, her tone near-hysterical, her hair all awry where she'd presumably been sleeping. 'Now, Casey, seriously! They need to find Millie! Now!'

Let Me Go

'What's going on, Harley?' I asked, leaping up. 'Has she been in touch with you? What's happened?'

'We have to find her!' she shrieked. 'We have to find her before he *kills* her!'

Chapter 17

I had never seen Harley so animated and determined. I jumped to my feet. 'What do you mean, love? Who will kill who? I don't understand.'

Two lobster-pink spots glowed bright on Harley's cheeks. '*Millie*!' she said. 'You know – *Millie*. My *sister*! Zar, her so-called boyfriend, will kill her. I know he will! We have to find her!'

I gently took the phone from her hands, expecting to see some sort of threatening message on the screen, but there was just a number at the top of a *recent calls* list.

'So, Millie has phoned you?' I asked her. 'Is this her number, love?'

'No!' Harley snapped, her voice getting more agitated by the second. 'It must be Zar's number. Zar! Her bastard boyfriend! She was trying to speak to me, I know she was! I heard her voice! And he must have stopped her. And now nothing. It's going straight to voicemail. Because he knows it's me now, doesn't he?

Let Me Go

We have to *find* her! Not just stand here doing *nothing*!' she finished.

Bastard boyfriend? Mike stood up too. 'Okay, okay, let's dial everything down a bit, okay? Harley, take a deep breath and calm down a bit, then tell us what's happened, why you think she's in danger, so that we can try to understand what's been happening, okay? And maybe help get to the bottom of it. Plan?'

For a moment I thought she might lash out at one or other of us, grab the phone out of my hand and make a bolt from the house, but though she was clearly as taut and as stretched out as a tightrope, her shoulders dropped a little and I could see she was thinking. Whatever had happened, she needed us on side right now.

'I do want to tell you,' she said, in a whisper. 'I've wanted to tell you for *such* a long time. But I was scared, and – oh, God, please, we need to find her. He'll *kill* her.'

'Come on, love,' I said, touching her lightly on the arm. However natural and instinctive it felt to try and comfort her, I knew better than to put my arm around her. 'Come and sit down, try and tell us all about it.'

To my relief she let me lead her to the sofa. Straight away, though, she lowered her head into her hands and started rocking back and forth, moaning, 'Nooo! Oh no, oh no, oh *no*!'

I sat close beside her. I still didn't want to touch her, but I did want her to know that I was there for her. As was Mike, who squatted down on the carpet in front of her. 'Deep breath,' he said. 'Now, what's been going on?'

She raised her head then. 'I don't *know*. I just know it was her. I heard her voice, I know I did—'

'And what did she say?'

'Just "Harley". Just, "Harley is that you? Are you there?" Then a noise and her saying no. Then a bang, then a sound like – like she was struggling. And I *know* it was him—'

'Zar?'

'Of course, Zar! Who else? He'll have taken the phone off her. We have to find her or he'll kill her, because he'll know she's called *me*. And that I'll tell. Don't you *see*?'

'Not quite,' Mike admitted. 'Tell what, Harley? What do you need to tell us?'

'*Everything*! God, I should have realised. I'm so *stupid*!' She looked at each of us in turn. 'Please, can't we just call the police? I'm not joking, I'm serious. It's his phone, I know it is. That's why he's not answering anymore, why it's going to voicemail.'

'And does the voicemail say it's him?'

'No, of *course* not. He's not *stupid*.' She leapt up again then. 'Please, we *have* to make them find her. They can do that. They have his number now, so surely they can do that?'

'Not as easily as all that,' Mike said, 'Not without a little more to go on. Do you know where they are? Where they're living, or anything?'

'And are you sure, love?' I added. 'What makes you think Zar will hurt her? From what I've heard—'

There were tears running down her face now and she

was wringing her hands; pulling one against the other as if trying to tug them from their wrists. 'Because I never *told*! Because nobody *knows*!' She was screeching now. 'Because he's a *monster*!'

'Okay,' I said, standing up again, catching Mike's eye. There was something chillingly credible about all this. 'There's clearly lots you need to tell us, but first, we need a plan to help Millie, don't we?'

Harley nodded, a big emphatic up-and-down movement. 'And I will tell, I promise. I will now. I'll tell everything. Even if it means Mum does get into trouble. If he hurts Millie, I will *never* forgive myself. I'll—'

'Okay, okay,' I said, trying to digest what she was saying. *I will tell*. So oddly childlike. So resolute. So scared. 'First things first, yes. Let's start with the details you know. You say you don't know where they are?' She shook her head. 'So, might anyone else know? Your mum, perhaps? A friend?'

'The kebab shop. His family. Someone *must* know where they're living. And Tessa might know something, mightn't she?'

Tessa Halliday, I thought wryly, who had actually met Zar and could not have sung his praises any more highly. But perhaps she would have. Because Harley *didn't tell*.

But tell what? I mentally rifled through my personal catalogue of misdemeanours. This child had been found on a bridge, intent on suicide. I could come up with all sorts but one thing seemed sure: that it was unlikely to be anything minor.

'Okay,' I said, glancing at the clock. Not too late yet. 'First off, I think I should call Tessa. And while I'm doing that, I think we could all use a coffee.'

Mike unbent and stretched. 'Okay, I'll do the honours. And Harley,' he added gently, 'we've got this, okay?'

I wasn't on the phone to Tessa for long. I'd anticipated a lot of humming and hawing and 'let's take a formal statement from her first' – which I'd planned to argue against vociferously. I'd retreated into the conservatory to make the call for that very reason. But I think she realised that I was not okay with any 'leave it with me' stuff and that my instinct was sound, that it was serious. That *I* was serious. In truth, I had no idea if Harley's sister was in any danger, but even if she wasn't, this was a major breakthrough moment, and though I'd never play fast and loose with the emergency services, what we had here was the potential to 'unlock' this desperate child, the positives of which could potentially far outweigh the negatives – the very worst of which could be her succeeding in killing herself.

And to do that, we needed to show Harley unequivocally that we did take her seriously, that Zar could well be a monster and that we'd do all we could to locate Millie.

And Tessa came good. Yes, she did know a little about Zar's family and she was confident Harley's mum might be able to add some detail too. 'And *I'll* call the police,' she said. 'You concentrate on Harley. Plus, it might help move things on a little quicker.' Which was a big plus, because we really didn't have a great deal to go on and despite Harley's confidence that the mobile phone number could locate Zar, I wasn't quite as confident; with mobile privacy laws being what they were, I wasn't sure that it would be much use at all. But what did I know? I'd only just worked out how to create something called an 'Instagram Story' – technology was doubtless light years ahead of me. But Tessa's family knowledge was another string to our bow. If Zar hadn't gone completely off-grid – and my hunch was he wouldn't have – we seemed to have a good chance of locating them. I truly hoped so.

I rang off, promising to let her know if Harley came up with anything else that might be useful, and returned to the living room, where Harley was huddled now, at the far end of the sofa, clutching a mug of coffee to her chest and looking like a ghost.

Mike handed me my coffee and I went over to sit down beside her. It struck me that this was the first time since she'd been with us that she'd actually sat on our sofa.

'Right,' I said, 'they are on to it. And they are confident they can find her. And while they do what they need to do, it's important that we know what we are dealing with. So, sweetie, what is it you need to tell?'

Chapter 18

She'd never known her dad, because she had only been three when he'd died, though it had always felt like his presence was everywhere. There was what he'd named her, for starters, which was such a cool name. Her friends at school were always envious. Grown-ups asked her about it. As far as she knew, she was the only Harley in the entire world.

Her big sister Millie was named after Harley-Davidsons too – they'd called her Millie after Milwaukee, which was the town in America where they first made them – but she was always glad (if in secret – she would never actually say so) that he'd saved the best name till she'd come along. It meant a lot to her that her dad had named her Harley.

His death had changed everything in an instant. In a heartbeat. It had snuffed him out and killed something in her mother as well. She had never known the happy times – had never ever *seen* her mother happy – but

Millie would often tell her stories about her daddy, so that's what he became for her: a story-book hero. Yes, he was dead, so she never felt his actual arms around her, but she knew he'd loved her – you could see it in the photos, which her mum had put everywhere – and because of that, she loved him as well.

And she carried a piece of him always. Millie told her the story once of how their mum and dad took her to America when she was little, a long time before Harley was born. They'd been to Disneyland, and her mum had bought her dad a Disneyland hoodie, and when he'd died, she never washed it because she wanted to keep the smell. But eventually she abandoned it and one night when Harley was crying, Millie gave it to her to have instead. 'It's Daddy's way of giving you a hug,' she'd said, 'so you know he's still watching over you.' Harley knew she would keep it for ever.

Her mum was sixteen when she'd had Millie and it was like she still was, so maybe their daddy wasn't watching over her. She'd never really worked, because their daddy took care of everything, so when he died there wasn't much she was qualified to do. And she wasn't really fit to work, in any case, and didn't seem to need to, because the drink and drugs took care of everything. Mostly her pain, which was the thing that had always mattered most. That she was in pain and didn't know what else to do. So by the time Harley was old enough to understand how the world worked, Harley's mum, in every important way, was Millie.

If Harley needed anything – clean underwear for school, something for tea, just a cuddle, her mum always said the same: 'Stop bothering me, for God's sake – go and ask your sister.'

They managed for a bit – a few years – supported by benefits and kindly neighbours, but when Harley was five, they were evicted from their home and rehoused to a tiny flat – saying goodbye to their little garden – and in an area where they knew absolutely no one. Harley had never felt so far away from everything and everyone she had ever known. So far away from Mr Hinds, from number five, who dropped chocolate bars through their letter box because he knew they never had enough to eat. So far from Mrs Lennox, from across the road, who'd bring a saucepan of stew round on Fridays. So far from Mrs Pearson, round the corner, who had a spaniel called Billy and would sometimes let her play with him in their garden. All those people who made her feel safe, as if she mattered, and who disappeared from her life at a stroke.

And though a kindly neighbour helped their mother enrol both girls in a local school and nursery, it was hard to make friends, because their mother didn't want to. She didn't want to do anything, or speak to anyone. She barely left the house. 'Go and find some friends then!' her mother would say. 'Who am I? Your fucking social secretary?'

Still, Millie was resourceful and determined, and very quick to learn, and she learned that, as a family, their days could be numbered; she knew they were talked about; that other grown-ups stared at them, that people wondered about them, and worried about them. And that a man might come along one day and take them away. 'You get it sorted, girl!' she would hear her mum screaming at Millie. And 'Keep that bloody kid quiet or you know what'll happen. They'll be knocking at this frigging door and taking the pair of you!'

'To a place called a children's home,' Millie told Harley if ever she asked what their mum meant. Which made Harley think of the Child Catcher in *Chitty Chitty Bang Bang*, which scared her, so she always did what her big sister told her. And with their mother barely able to lift herself off the sofa most days, Millie, who knew the best way to keep her family together was to 'stay under the radar', did just about everything that needed to be done. She took Harley to school every day – at least, till she was old enough to take herself – did the housework, the shopping, the cooking, the cleaning, and, though they lived hand to mouth and were frightened all the time, she coped just about enough so that the family were left alone, more or less, by an already overstretched social services.

And then, one day, everything changed.

Harley was nine when Zar arrived in her life. At first like a bear – like a big, friendly bear – who was sitting in the kitchen when she came home from school one day, and making her mum laugh, which was strange, because her mum didn't laugh at all. *Ever*. Zar had a beard, and a car, and smoked funny-smelling cigarettes. Millie explained to her that Zar was her boyfriend.

She had other words for him too: he was 'the love of her life', he was her 'rock', he was going to be their 'saviour'. Harley wasn't sure quite how he was going to save anyone – and did they even want 'saving'? (By now, she was used to the rhythms of their existence and notions of being saved came with the term 'social services' attached to them – the spectre of being taken away still burned bright in her mind.)

But 'save' them was what Zar seemed to be destined to do. His real name was Hamzar, and he was very well known locally, because he ran the Turkish kebab shop a few streets away from them. And everyone, it seemed, really loved him. 'Oh, Zar,' people said, 'he's the salt of the earth, that one', which Harley took to mean, having wondered about it, that he looked after his family, that he was hard-working, kind and good, that – this bit she found out a little while later – people had a lot of time for him on account of him being so decent in supporting his girlfriend's troubled, struggling family so well. 'Shame there aren't more like him,' Millie reported to her one day, beaming, having been told it by the lady in the chemists.

Most amazingly, he made their mother smile again. Harley knew it was partly because he showered her with shopping, fags and booze, and partly because he called her 'Millie-mum', which made her giggle. But it was also because for the first time in what had felt like for ever, the family didn't struggle any more. And when Zar started staying over, first for days, then for weeks, then what felt like for ever, no one batted an eyelid about how old he seemed for Millie, because Millie seemed so grown-up herself.

Harley was growing up too. And, in growing up, she began to grow fearful. She never said anything – not to Millie, and definitely not to her mother – but she felt uncomfortable living with a bear in the house. It was great not having to worry whether there would be anything for tea, but a bear on the landing, hardly dressed, was a little scary, and the sound of a bear doing things in Millie's bedroom made her stomach lurch and her mind fill with horrible pictures; night after night she'd have to sleep with her pillow clamped around her ears.

She also, increasingly, missed her big sister. When she'd been little, Millie had been the one to tuck her up in bed, and tell her stories, and, as she'd grown, been the one who she could confide her darkest fears to, or just chat, under the covers, about stuff. Now though, she was often up in her room – sometimes before it was even dark – locked away with Zar, and Harley, who cried herself to sleep most nights now, would pray that the noises she heard coming from her sister didn't mean that Zar was hurting her. For what seemed like the first time in for ever, Harley felt abandoned by Millie and understood what it felt like to be lonely.

Her mum, meanwhile, did what she'd always done best – sit on the sofa, in the living room, watching-but-not-watching the telly, a drink in her hand, the ashtray at her elbow. She still loved Zar – 'Oh, *you*,' she'd say, punching him playfully when he teased her, which was often – but she was more interested, clearly, in the comforts he'd provided and, now she had them, she was an even more hazy and disconnected presence.

And the more it went on, the more Harley worried. She worried that she'd come home from school one day to find her mother asleep (she was usually asleep when Harley came home from school), but that she wasn't asleep, she was dead. She worried that Millie, ever more there-but-not-there for her, was increasingly not going to school. She worried mostly (and she didn't tell anyone about this, because who would listen?) that Zar, who did not officially live with the family, saw himself as the king of their little kingdom.

It was around then that he started to rule it as well, with what Harley realised (she would read in the school library, often) was called an 'iron fist'.

The first time she knew it was when she'd come home from school one day to find Zar and Millie in the kitchen, him shouting, her sobbing, and what looked like all their dinner plates smashed to bits on the floor. 'Just do the fucking washing-up, okay!' were the first words she'd heard as she'd come in the front door.

Millie was crying. She was always crying these days. Normally she hid it – she didn't realise Harley knew already – but tonight she didn't even seem to notice Harley there. 'I'm sorry, Zar, I really am,' she sobbed. 'I promise, I'll try to be better.'

'You fucking do that!' he yelled, making Harley cower in the kitchen doorway. 'You need to pull your weight in this house. You live like pigs!'

They'd made friends again, later – he'd even helped her sweep up all the debris – and that night she could hear them doing stuff in Millie's bedroom for half the night. But the look on his face as he'd raged at her sister was one she wouldn't easily forget. So from that day, despite him being a friendly bear again in the morning, she knew to be wary of his rages. And that she needed to be a grown-up and help Millie around the house more.

And his rages became just like their mother's drunken dozing: a fact of life they had no choice but to work around. And if he got really cross he wouldn't just throw things, he would punish the girls physically and take pleasure in doing so, taking off his thick, oily belt with a flourish and hitting Millie and Harley with it, on their arms and legs and buttocks, creating bruises so livid that neither dared to go to school in case somebody saw them. Sometimes, to make them learn their lesson and their 'place' in his kingdom, he would disappear for days without any warning, leaving them without food or money to buy any. Those were the only times she really felt her mother's presence in the house, because, deprived of booze and fags, she'd cry too.

'You did this!' her mum would scream at poor Millie, spit flying. 'See what you've done? You've driven him away now! What is *wrong* with you, for God's sake? Now we *all* have to suffer!' And Harley felt confused; she simply couldn't understand why their mum thought it was all her sister's fault.

But it was the effect on Millie that distressed and puzzled Harley the most. She would mope around in Zar's absences, crying about how much she loved and needed him, and when he returned – usually bearing ridiculously large bunches of flowers and presents – she would be so happy to have him back that she'd cry all over again. And if Harley ever dared to suggest that he was bad to be shouting at them and hitting them, Millie would rail at her little sister for being so childish and ungrateful and threaten her with the children's home if she told.

'Don't spoil things,' she'd plead, 'or you'll ruin it for all of us. Zar will leave us and then you *know* where we'll end up!'

But it was when Harley was ten, not even yet in high school, that she realised that life had the capacity for becoming even worse. She knew it the moment she woke up one night in her bed to find Zar climbing into it with her.

'Stop being such a baby,' he'd whisper, with his foul smoky breath. 'Your sister doesn't make all this fuss, she *really likes it*.' Which was an idea that frightened Harley even more. That and the pain. It felt as if she would never be able to walk again.

Let Me Go

The brutal sex, laced with terror (he assured her he would kill both Millie and her mother if she told them, and she believed him), became a regular small-hours occurrence. But as Harley loved and depended on her sister much more than her mother, she submitted to it. She didn't know what else to do. After all (as he told her again and again), if he left, which he'd have to if Harley spoke to anyone, her mum would be arrested and locked away in prison, and the girls would be taken too and placed in different children's homes.

The small-hours visits were still happening when Harley started high school and when she turned eleven, Zar bought her a present. It was all wrapped up in pretty paper, with a bow on the top, and though she hated him more than she thought possible to hate anyone, it was a mobile phone so she was never *not* going to accept it.

'It's on a contract,' Zar said, 'and I'm paying it, remember. And will keep doing so as long as you don't piss me off and are a *good girl*.'

Now she was eleven and had a bus pass, and could sense a future, she dreamed often of running away and having a phone made that dream even more of a possibility. But by now a solitary and introverted figure, she found it impossible to make friends. The other girls would laugh at her for being so odd – what kind of girl was she, that she wasn't interested in boys, or clothes, or make-up? The only friend she did make was an odd girl in her tutor group who, similarly friendless, told her a good way to make yourself better when you felt bad was to cut your arms with a blade out of an old-fashioned razor. So began Harley's self-harming.

One night, after a visit in her bedroom from Zar, Harley was so upset that she took a razor from the side of the bath, locked herself in the bathroom and started cutting her arms till she drew blood. Surprised at the rush of relief the act brought her, her alone times in the bathroom became a regular ritual to make the nights of violence and violation more bearable.

To make her more bearable even to herself. She hated that she let Zar do the things he did to her, and, as well as making her feel better, feel more in control, punishing her body felt right and felt good; made it look as disgusting on the outside as she felt on the inside.

But to live such a life was increasingly unbearable, and with the frequency and severity of Harley's self-harming growing, one day, at school, it was finally spotted. And once reported, a teacher removed Harley from class and took her to the medical room. 'I need to see your arms,' she said, and not at all unkindly. 'We're here to help you,' she added. 'It's okay.'

But it was not okay.

'Harley, sweetheart, you have to tell me why you've been doing this to yourself,' the teacher had told her. 'You won't get into any trouble, but, darling, you need to tell me. It's absolutely nothing to be ashamed about.'

But she was ashamed. And she was frightened. If she told, what about Mum? Would Mum go to prison for letting Zar do what he did to her? Would she be taken off, all alone, to a children's home?

So she didn't tell, and she thought it would all be alright, but then a lady arrived one day when they were dishing up tea. A stranger from what she called social services.

Zar was all about. Being nice. Saying yes, I do my best. Yes, I do most of the cooking – which was a lie. Millie did it. 'I come from a large catering family,' he said, 'so when I cook, it's often like I'm feeding a small army.'

The social services lady smiled and laughed. She seemed to think Zar was funny, especially when he asked her to stay to tea. 'Oh, I can't,' she said. 'My husband is quite the cook too, actually – much as I'd love to. Mmm … it smells amazing!'

Harley thought she'd never ever forget that conversation.

But then the lady turned to her. Started asking about her cutting herself. And then it all became even more unreal. Her mum, cooing and fussing and so obviously drunk, and saying, 'Oh, oh, my baby! Oh, she misses her dad so much. I don't think she's ever really got over it, to be honest. Have you been having bad dreams again, Harley-belle?'

It was like a bad dream in itself. And why didn't the lady even notice how drunk her mum was? And why was Zar telling the lady that she'd always had nightmares and how they all worried about her such a lot?

The lady gave them a list of to-do things. To make an appointment with their GP (did they even *have* a GP?) to see if he felt she needed 'referring' for extra help. And to make sure all her teachers were aware that she was 'struggling' and a promise to say the very moment she ever had a thought about cutting herself. 'Harley's at that age now,' she said, 'where she really needs to be able to express her emotions and, well, teenagers tend to be able to speak to a third party better. The family is often too close to the problem.'

'Yes, Harley-belle,' Zar said, 'you must make sure you do that. Fancy doing all this and none of us *knowing*.' And the look in his eyes as he said that made her terrified. So terrified that she didn't want the lady to leave. Which made her start crying and she couldn't seem to stop, despite knowing Zar's eyes were boring into her.

The lady frowned. 'Is there anywhere I can have a quick word with Harley alone, please?' she asked her mother. 'It's just procedure, you know, when a report like this has been made and it should only take a few minutes. Yes? And then I can go and leave you in peace to get on with that *delicious*-looking meal.'

It was Zar who showed both of them to the back room, so he could pinch the skin under Harley's arms as he did so. 'I'll leave you both in here,' he said to the lady, 'and, Harley, if you need me, just shout. Okay, sweetheart?'

Harley knew then and there that she wouldn't tell. If she told, he would kill her. He might kill Millie too.

'I just miss my dad sooo much,' she said. 'And sometimes' – and she was sobbing with terror so the lies were really easy – 'it just gets too much and I can't stop myself', when what she really wanted to say was *please take Zar away, please just take him away*, but she couldn't.

'And what will you do if you get overwhelmed like this again, Harley?' the woman asked, very gently. 'Because, you know, that might happen, and you need to have strategies.'

'I will tell someone,' she promised. 'I will tell someone at school.'

But of course she wouldn't. It was a lie. Her whole life was a lie. But anything was better than telling the truth. That would only get her mother sent to jail and she would be sent to a children's home.

After that, Zar made her life hell. He was livid and threatened that if anyone else came to the house, he wouldn't just stop at killing her. 'I will bury you alive,' he assured her as he hit her with his belt, 'somewhere no one will ever find you.'

This was terrifying enough, but there was worse still to come. Shortly afterwards, Millie told her that she knew about the sex, and though for an instant Harley thought her sister was going to do something to stop it, she explained that it was important that Harley understood that, for Zar and his family, this was normal. That in lots of religions – like 'the Mormons', she told her – it was just what they did and that it was important that she learned to 'play the game'. If she couldn't, her sister added, then she would have little choice but to go away with Zar and make a life somewhere else.

Something happened to Harley that evening: she discovered rage. Now it was clear that this life was the one her sister had chosen, she couldn't see a point in continuing such an existence. And with nothing to lose, she also found sufficient courage to tell her mother that she was going to report what was *really* going on the very minute she got into school the next day. 'I can't bear to live like this anymore, Mum,' she told her. 'And our only way out is for me to *tell*.'

It was the biggest mistake of her life.

'You just dare, Harley,' her mum warned. 'You keep your trap closed.'

And when she woke up the next day she knew her mum had betrayed her. Because Zar had gone. And her beloved sister had as well. All she'd left was a note, on her laptop, which she'd left behind: *For you. Love you, Harlz xx*. And that was all.

Her mum was on the sofa, sleeping. It was like she *lived* on the sofa these days.

'Where's Millie?' she cried, frantically shaking her and shaking her. 'Where's Millie? Mum, wake *up*! All her things are gone!'

Her mum stretched and yawned. 'And so's our fucking meal ticket,' she drawled, lighting a cigarette. 'I told you this would happen, you stupid girl.'

Let Me Go

'You mean you *told* Millie?' Harley couldn't believe what she was hearing.

'Of course I told her! What else was I going to fucking do? You go blabbing to some teacher and we're all going to cop it! So, yeah, they've gone. And it's all your fucking fault.'

Stunned that her sister could abandon her the way she did, Harley was now paralysed by indecision. Though her relief at Zar's departure from their home was profound, she had now lost her sister and, without her, what on earth was she to do? Should she still tell a teacher? Her instinct was yes, but with the state her mother was now in, Zar's threats still rang true.

She was only thirteen; she'd be packed off to a children's home, surely? And her mother to – where? What would happen to her if she told someone the truth? Would she really be sent to prison? She dare not risk it.

The next few days passed in a blur of misery and recriminations. Her mother blamed her for 'destroying everything' and sank even further. One day, Harley even came home from school to find her in bed still, lying passed out in a pool of her own urine. And when the alcohol ran out, she just took more pills and Harley dared not leave her alone to go to school.

That was the first time she had thought about killing herself.

But a few days later some relief came in the shape of a letter; a wodge of money, quite a lot of it, and a note from her sister, telling her Zar had at least agreed to keep paying the rent and the contract for her precious phone.

The money helped. Filled her tummy, and made her mum scream a bit less at her, and gave her hope that her sister hadn't completely abandoned her, but it couldn't ever fill the hole in her soul.

Millie also called the following week, and then again, a week later, telling Harley that she was sorry, but she was happy, and that she wasn't coming back. That she was going to visit soon, to check they were okay, but simply couldn't bear to return to her old life.

Harley cried and cried and cried. Was it her fault?

No, Millie told her, it wasn't her fault. It was nobody's fault, it just was what it was. As if there was nothing to be done but accept that she'd left and was not coming back again. 'Speak to someone,' she told Harley, 'about getting help for Mum. Tell a teacher. Tell a neighbour. Tell someone in authority. Get that woman back from social services and ask if she can help.'

But wouldn't that mean they'd *still* send Harley to a children's home? On her *own*? *No*, Millie promised her. At least, not necessarily. But Harley looked at her mum and knew Millie was wrong. If she was the social services lady, would *she* let her stay?

And within a couple of months, Millie's phone calls stopped coming. As did the bits of money, and though her mobile phone contract hadn't been cancelled – her precious lifeline to her sister – Millie had also disappeared from social media. And stopped responding to Harley's increasingly desperate texts.

Feeling truly abandoned now, Harley didn't know what to do. And when a letter came, informing them that they were going to be evicted, she could not see a way out for either her or her mother that wouldn't make her hellish life even more hellish.

That night was the watershed. With nothing left to live for, why not simply die? She didn't believe in much, but she did believe this: if she died, she would be with her father. So she took her favourite photo of the hero she'd never known, and headed to the bridge over the motorway.

Chapter 19

'Mum's going to be sent to prison now, isn't she?'

It was almost ten by the time Harley had finished telling us her story, the coffee long gone and the room in near-darkness, lit only by the light coming from the muted television.

I thought of all the ways her mother had broken the law. Quite apart from the manifest chronic neglect, if what Harley had told us was true, she had done absolutely nothing about sustained abuse of a child – her own daughter – that had been going on for years, under her own roof. She wouldn't be the first woman to have done so and she wouldn't be the last. By any yardstick, she was bang to rights and they'd throw the book at her. What had I overheard her say to Harley? *Do you want me put in prison?* She must be living, I realised, in a state of great fear.

Which would naturally lead me to think *absolutely, and she should be!* To let something like that happen to her own child – her *two* children – and do nothing to get them justice, to see the perpetrator behind bars – it almost beggared belief. But then I thought about the fact that she was broken too. Had been broken for many years, by the sound of it, taking refuge from her grief in booze and drugs. And clearly to an extent that had half-destroyed her. Life as a foster carer had opened my eyes to a lot of things and one of them was that there was never a straightforward answer to the question of who were the victims and who were the guilty. You didn't have to venture far into a 'guilty' person's past to find that, at one time, they'd been victims as well. No, in this case, not a victim of abuse, as far as I knew, but the victim of circumstance; of a tragic loss which she'd never got over and, without a family to support her – Harley said she'd never known any other family, because her mum ran away from home to be with her father – had clearly overwhelmed her. Life was full of blurred lines and I always tried to keep that in mind. Recriminations rarely helped anything along.

'I don't know,' I told Harley. 'I genuinely can't say what will happen, because I genuinely don't know what's going to happen next. I imagine the police will want to interview her about Zar, which is obviously important, but, other than that, I really don't know. But whatever happens, they will take account of the fact that your mum is very sick. Has been sick for a long time. And very vulnerable. I would hope that, now we know the

225

truth, she will be able to get some help. As will you,' I added.

'I don't care about *me*,' she said, 'I just want them to find Millie.'

'Well, *I* care about you. We all care about you. And we're going to make sure you get all the help you need to help you come to terms with all this.'

'I don't need help,' she insisted. 'I just need them to find Millie!'

'And they will. And the very minute they do, they will call me. Tessa's promised.'

'But right now we all need to get to bed, I think,' Mike added.

I looked over at my husband, who'd been sitting across from us in the armchair, a shadowy figure lit only by the light from the table lamp. He'd said almost nothing while Harley told us her story – the only indication that he was listening, and taking in the catalogue of horrors, had been the set of his mouth and the tic in his jaw. We were both inured now, to an extent, to hearing stories like Harley's, but it wasn't often that he had a ringside seat. Mostly he was at work and it was me kids disclosed to, so he'd get an edited, slightly sanitised, version from me later on.

So I felt for him. Felt the revulsion I knew he was feeling. Understood how, in his male way, that feeling was so powerful. How the all-too-vivid picture of Zar Harley had painted would be affecting him in such a physical way. I knew he'd think of his own daughter and of his granddaughters too. How he'd be thinking, even if he'd never ever do it, that he'd like to pulverise Zar with his bare fists.

I could see all of that and my heart really went out to him. He needed his sleep not just because we were all by now exhausted, but because in a few hours his bedside alarm would be going off and he'd have to get up, like normal, have his shower, just like normal, then get in his car and drive to work, and *be normal*.

He was good at compartmentalising – the family, the fostering, the day job – but I knew trying to do that tomorrow would be hard. He heard things, and experienced things, his colleagues mostly didn't. How could it ever not be hard?

'Mike's right, love,' I said, standing up and stretching the stiffness from my tired limbs. 'I know it's going to be hard to sleep, but it's getting late and we at least need to try. And I promise you that my phone will be right next to me, on my bedside, and I will wake you immediately if I get any news in the night.'

'I don't think I can bear to go to bed,' she said. 'Can't I just stay down here for now?'

'You need your sleep, love,' Mike said. 'Come on, let's all hit the hay now. We're all going to feel better once we've had a bit of sleep.'

To which Harley burst into a fresh bout of tears.

'Oh, sweetheart,' I said, going back to sit down beside her and putting my arm around her. 'I know … it's all so hard … shh. Come on, let's head up, shall we?'

She shook her head. 'I just don't think I can bear to go back upstairs. To that *room* …' I felt her shudder. And the penny dropped immediately.

Of course she couldn't bear it. Because of what it represented. To us it was just a room – our third, 'fostering' bedroom. To Harley it was a place where she had existed in a living hell.

I looked at Mike. 'Go on, you head up, love. Get your head down.' Then, once he'd gone, to Harley: 'That's fine, love. More than fine. I understand completely. Tell you what, let's make a bed up for you down here.'

Still she sobbed. 'I'm so sorry I've caused all this trouble.'

I put both arms around her now, drew her close and hugged her tightly. 'Shh … you mustn't think like that, sweetie. You haven't caused any of this. Not a single bit of it. *None* of this is your fault. It's important that you understand that. You've done nothing wrong, you've been *done* wrong. By all sorts of people. But now they're going to find Millie. Because you did the right thing and *told*. Which means we can fix things, okay? Both for you and for Millie. Now, how about I go up and fetch a duvet and some pillows? Mike's right. You're going to feel so much better once you've slept. And I'm going to stay right here beside you till you do.'

'With your phone.'

'With my phone.'

* * *

Let Me Go

It was almost one before I slipped, as quietly as I could, into bed. But though I thought Mike was fast asleep, I felt his hand reach out to squeeze mine beneath the covers.

'All well?' he murmured.

'All well,' I told him.

Because though I had no way of knowing if all would be well with Harley – she had such a long difficult road ahead of her – for the moment, at least, all really *was* well. She had let me hug her. Let me offer her basic physical human comfort. Such a simple thing, to be hugged, but such an important one too. To accept comfort from a stranger, given all that she had suffered, all she'd been through. Whatever else was true, that really felt like a breakthrough.

Chapter 20

Tessa called to let us know they had found Millie at around seven the following morning, just after Mike left for work. She was currently billeted at the home of an emergency foster carer, and though the task of finding Zar was still ongoing, she was apparently safe and well, and very keen to get back in touch with her little sister.

But that could wait. Harley was still fast asleep on the sofa, so despite the promise I'd made to her the previous evening, I didn't wake her; I knew she was going to have a few long days ahead of her.

I took both my phone and my coffee out into the conservatory.

'I have a very great deal to report back to you as well,' I told Tessa. 'Though right now, I'm not sure I can think straight, let alone anything else. But trust me, it's going to be a *very* long email.'

'They're the kind I like best,' she said, laughing. 'Nothing like coming into work and seeing three-figure numbers in my inbox, especially knowing that at least one of them's got a priority flag beside and is going to be ten pages long. That's why I opted for a career in social services!'

I laughed too. I was pleased that we could joke with one another like this. I didn't know how long my relationship with Tessa Halliday was going to last now, but it felt good to know that we'd drawn a line in the sand after a fractious few weeks, and that if our paths crossed again, which they obviously might, it would be without any residual rancour. It had been a stressful few weeks for her as well.

'Ditto fostering,' I agreed. 'I just *live* for the paperwork. Though right now I'm almost as eager to hear how the police managed to track her down.'

'Oh, they didn't, in the end,' she said. 'She found them.'

It turned out that it had been quite a night. Millie's aborted call to Harley had been the result of an encounter with a downstairs neighbour, which had led to a visit from the police.

'Lots of rows, lots of arguments all the time,' Tessa explained. 'And the man, apparently sick of being disturbed by them all the time, decided he'd had enough – he was also concerned about Millie's welfare, obviously – and called the police, asking if they'd go round and check on them. Which they did and though Hamzar managed to convince them that all was well between them, as soon as they'd gone, he apparently turned on

Millie, accusing her of being the one who had called them. Which is a bit rich, it turns out, since it transpires that he pretty much had control of her mobile phone. I think there's quite a can of worms still to be opened in that respect.'

'From what Harley tells me, there will be more than a can,' I said. 'More like an entire wormery. Anyway, sorry, go on, we can get to all that later. What happened then?'

'It seems there was a bit of a scuffle in the living room, during which he apparently smashed Millie's mobile, but Millie managed to make him lose his balance, during which he dropped his own, and she had the presence of mind to make a grab for it. She ran into the bathroom then, and locked the door, and was able to dial Harley's number, before he managed to shoulder the door hard enough to break the lock and get it back off her.

'I'm not quite sure about all the ins and outs that happened after that, but the neighbour was obviously privy to all the shouts and bangings and got back in touch with the police again, reporting that he'd seen Hamzar subsequently drive off, but that when he went up to their flat, fearful now that Millie might be hurt, he could get no answer when he knocked at the door.'

'She's not hurt, is she?'

'No, she's fine. Badly bruised and shaken but nothing she wasn't used to, by all accounts. She apparently told the woman from EDT that he beat her up regularly.'

'Harley's said the same,' I said. 'God, he really is a monster. So where was she?'

'Still in the flat at that point. Busy packing a bag and too afraid to answer the door. She sneaked out when all was quiet an hour or so later and took a bus to the nearest police station – she had no phone of course, so she couldn't make a call.'

'So where is she? I mean, where were they living? Is it a way away?'

She named a town about thirty miles away, a place near the coast. 'Where he's been running a kebab shop owned by one of his uncles. Or rather was. By the time our lot got to the flat – they'd traced Hamzar's phone to there by this time – there was nobody there.'

'So they did do it via the phone number?'

'Yes, they use the GPS, don't they? But it's no help to them now, because he obviously took the SIM out and left it there. Millie getting through to Harley on his mobile was the catalyst, apparently. He obviously realised the game might be up. Anyway, he scarpered and once they got word through that Millie had already presented herself at the local police station, they went straight over there to interview her, so they now have more to go on. It's only going to be a matter of time before he's found. At which point, I trust they'll throw the bloody book at him.'

'The whole bloody library,' I said with feeling.

'Anyway, how are you fixed today? I'm obviously going to need to come over and have a bit of a chat with Harley. How is she doing?'

At which point I heard a noise behind me. I turned

around to see her standing, bleary-eyed and anxious, in the conservatory doorway. I smiled, lifted a thumb in the air, smiled again.

'She's going to be fine now,' I told Tessa.

Chapter 21

In the end, both Tessa and Christine came over – and with Mike and Tyler both absent (there was a football match, involving a new second-time father, which needed watching) – we had a proper girly gathering in the living room. They stayed only an hour (which was enough, because Harley had had such a stressful twenty-four hours) both to fill her in about Millie, who they promised she'd be able to talk to very soon, and to explain what was going to happen next. They also explained that, though they'd spoken to her mum, they thought it best, since she was poorly, if Harley didn't speak to her herself at the moment, at least till the dust around Millie and Zar had all settled. Which was all a bit vague, a bit of a fudge, a bit woolly, but I knew it was important that all parties be interviewed separately, and that Harley's mum, particularly, given what we knew now, couldn't influence Harley in any way.

And she was fine with that. When Christine gently asked her if she was okay not speaking to her mum for a bit, she said, 'Fine, I don't want her shouting at me anyway. I just don't want her to have to go to prison because I told.'

About which Tessa was, thankfully, able to reassure her. 'Your mum won't go to prison,' she said. 'I can tell you that definitely. And it's important that you understand that *nothing* you say when the police come to talk to you will make things worse for your mother in *any* way. They are only interested in Zar, in what you can tell them about him, so that when they find him, they will know everything they need to. So don't be scared. Don't think that there's anything you *can't* say. Tell them everything you can remember, okay?'

And she would, I knew, because they would make sure of it. There was a world of difference between our jobs, caring for this abused, frightened teenager, and the task the police had, which was to gather as much information as they could, from all involved, so they could decide whether there was a case for prosecution. Because, right now, Zar was innocent till proven guilty. And that would remain the case until they had amassed sufficient evidence to actually charge him with his crimes.

So I knew Harley was in for a much tougher time when she told the police some of the things she'd told us. They would want every little detail, no matter how painful, and I knew from past experience – very recent past experience – that they delved very deep and into the most personal places. With this in mind, when I'd been told that a special officer would be coming round to take her statement the following day, I decided I would have to prepare her.

Since the disclosure everything had changed. It was like a cloud had been lifted, not just from over Harley, but over all of us. No longer was I dropping food off outside a closed bedroom door and praying that I'd catch sight of our silent lodger. Now, Harley was up early, joining me for breakfast, and then pottering around downstairs with me till lunchtime. She would go on her laptop in my presence, in the dining room, and even logged into her school website. Whether it would go on being her school website was another matter altogether, because who knew where she would eventually end up, but that was for another day. It just pleased me no end that she did.

I left it till the morning of the visit. The plainclothes detective, a Sam Donohoe, who specialised in interviewing abused children, was due to be with us at two. So I broached the coming interview over lunch.

It was a thrown-together, whatever's-in-the-fridge kind of salad; and a novelty in itself, to be sharing meals with her at our dining-room table. She'd not eaten a meal at *any* table for a month!

'So,' I said, 'you feeling up to this? Anything you want to ask me before the lady gets here? It might be a little bit of a tough ride for you today.'

She looked at me anxiously. 'But you'll be here?'

'Yes, of course I'll be here. Right beside you, so you don't need to worry about that. I just want you to be prepared that she might ask you things that might feel, well, a little uncomfortable to answer. Things that me, or Tessa, or Christine, never did. Things that might make you feel embarrassed, or upset. But she has to ask, because it's important that the police properly understand what Zar did to you. It's their job.'

Harley's cheeks began to redden. 'You mean like the sex stuff?' I nodded. 'What sort of things? What sort of things will she want me to say?'

I started to feel embarrassed for her myself now. She was *thirteen*. I didn't even know if she'd started her periods. 'I'm not absolutely certain, obviously, but, yes, definitely about the sex stuff. Everything else as well, of course, but yes, she will definitely ask you questions about Zar forcing you to have sex, but, love, she might also ask you things that might shock you a little – like did you want him to do it, did you ever try to stop him and what sorts of things did the two of you talk about. I know it sounds awful' – I could tell by her expression that she thought that as well – 'but they have to know, because, when they find Zar and question him, he will probably try to paint a very different picture, try to suggest that you encouraged him, that sort of thing. That's why it's so important they have a really detailed account from you.'

'Oh my God!' Harley gasped. 'Like they'd even *think* I'd want that doing to me. It's disgusting!'

'I know, love, I know. I'm sure you can't even bear to *think* about it, let alone have to talk about, and especially to a stranger. It's no wonder you kept it bottled up inside for so long.'

I could see her mind working then. 'But what if they don't believe me? What if they catch Zar and he tells them I *liked* what he did to me? What if they believe him instead of me? You don't know him. He makes everyone think he's not what he is. Nobody realises he's a monster. I've *seen* it. Millie knew and she still *loved* him. He's *evil*.'

'You don't need to worry about that, love,' I told her. 'They know what he's like. Millie will have told them what he's done to her. And they already know what you've been through as well. They have all of that evidence already, they just need to hear things from your perspective too. That's why, when the lady asks you things that make you feel anxious or embarrassed, you have to take a deep breath, gather up all your courage, and tell her the things she needs to hear from you. Like I say, it will be tough, but just remember why you're doing it. For you, of course, but also for Millie. So neither of you ever have to worry about him ever again.'

She nodded. 'Okay.' Then was silent for a moment. 'I nearly told you,' she said, finally. 'That day when you shouted at me by the park. I nearly plucked up the courage because I thought I was going to burst if I didn't. But I couldn't find enough of it, I could never find enough of it. That's my problem. I worked it out. I'm not brave enough.'

'Oh, sweetheart,' I told her. 'You have been *incredibly* brave.'

She shook her head. 'No, I haven't, because if I had, I wouldn't be here, would I?'

Which floored me for a moment. I didn't know quite what to say. Then it hit me. 'Well, in that case, I am really, really glad of it. But I wouldn't see it that way – you know, that you weren't being brave. That was just your brain trying to tell you that life *was* worth living. That whatever part of you made you think you had to die was thinking all wrong.' I tapped my head with my fork. 'Clever things, brains.'

'Mine wasn't. Well, even if it was, it was very, very scary. It was sometimes like I didn't have any control over anything. I'd get this noise in my head, this buzz, this sort of pain. Like *now* was the time. Like I had to find somewhere and just *do* it. It was like having this whole conversation going on inside my head. And then I'd get to wherever and I just *couldn't* do it. And it wasn't about Millie. I really thought I was never going to see her again. And it wasn't even about Zar. I never thought about Zar, I wouldn't allow him in my head. I'd just want to make the buzzing, the horrible pain go away. And then it would, and I'd be scared, and I didn't want to do it. But I didn't know what *else* to do.'

'A cry for help, then,' I suggested. 'Even if you didn't know it.'

She surprised me again then, by shaking her head. 'It really wasn't,' she said. 'I didn't think anyone could help me. I just wanted the buzzing – the pressure, you know?

– in my head to go away. But when it came to it, every time, I just could make myself.'

I wasn't sure if pressing the point was going to help her, but I couldn't stop myself. I just so badly wanted to be able to understand. 'You came dangerously close,' I said gently, 'when you tried to hang yourself in that toilet. And then from that tree.'

Again, she shook her head. 'The lead snapped because I yanked it off. I was petrified of suffocating. *Terrified*. And I thought then that perhaps it would all stop—' She put her hands to her head. 'The endless *noise*. But then it just started all over again. And I didn't know how to stop it. How to make it go away. That was help I *did* want. To help me find the courage to actually do it. That's when I started going on all those stupid, *stupid* forums.'

I got that, I understood. She must have felt so distressed, so despairing, so isolated by the secrets she was convinced she had to keep – it was no wonder she reached out for help in that way. And found yet more darkness. Truly terrifying. Enough to make her try again, and come even closer.

I reached a hand across the table to her, placed it over hers and squeezed it. 'Promise me something, Harley. That you'll never go anywhere near those again.'

She shook her head. Shuddered. 'Never. Never, *never*.'

* * *

It was good to clear the air a bit, delve a little into Harley's psyche, but I knew the interview would still be traumatic. The term PTSD is in common usage these days everywhere, but it's more often used in relation to returning soldiers than to scared, abused thirteen-year-old girls. But that was just how I was sure it must have felt. She was having to relive so many horrors.

Sam was gentle and warm, but had to do what she had to do. And after easing into the interview with a few less inflammatory questions, she was soon into the territory I'd been braced for. Did Harley like him at any point? Did she encourage him in any way, even if she hadn't meant to? Did she accept gifts from him which might have made him think she liked him even if she didn't? Did she feel grateful to him for helping keep her family together? How did she see him? Like a big brother? Possibly a kind of boyfriend at any point? Did he regularly see her around the house in her nightclothes or undressed? Was it possible that any of her memories might be wrong? What did she think of the possibility that Hamzar might suggest she was making it all up because she was jealous that he was her older sister's boyfriend? That she wanted to punish him for Millie deciding to leave home?

Most of these she answered in a flat, but firm monotone. Though now and then there would be flashes of hostility and temper, which the officer took with long-practised equanimity. 'I'm not trying to be awkward, Harley, or make you feel even worse than you do already, but if this goes to court, and of course we hope it does, and if Hamzar says he hasn't done anything wrong, then you may be asked to testify. To tell the court exactly what he did. Do you know what that means?'

Harley nodded slowly. 'I've seen it on TV,' she said. 'It means a judge might ask me some questions under oath and I have to tell the truth. But I might not have to do it in front of everyone.' She looked from one of us to the other. 'Is that right?'

Sam smiled and patted Harley on the leg. 'You got it, kiddo, but even hidden behind a screen, Hamzar will have a solicitor – that's someone he hires to stick up for his side of things, and that solicitor will question your statement and try to make it look not so bad so that his client doesn't get into trouble, so I'm just asking you some of the questions that the solicitor might ask you. And he might try to suggest you're not telling the truth. So you need to be absolutely sure about your answers and just tell the truth, okay?'

It went on much the same as this and by the time it had ended I could see that Harley was shattered. She asked if she could go and have a nap and I nodded. Though not in her bedroom. By now we'd transferred the put-you-up bed into the conservatory. It was cosy in there and, until she left us, that was where she'd stay. 'Course you can, lovey,' I said, 'and I'll give you a shout when tea's ready.'

* * *

'I'm sorry if that was a bit brutal,' the officer said after Harley had left us. 'But I want to be sure she's strong enough to give evidence if it's needed. Fingers crossed, it won't be. Hopefully, once we catch him, he'll see the strength of the case we have against him and plead guilty. Or his lawyer will see it, more to the point.'

'Any news on that yet?' I asked.

'We're making progress. We'll flush him out, don't you worry.'

'And Millie? Has she given you her statement?'

'*Ohhh*, yes,' she said, in a way that felt very reassuring. 'Quite the gentleman, our Hamzar is. Not. We have a pretty full picture, so we're confident where this is going. She's also confirmed that Harley did tell her about the late-night visits to her room. Horrible business for her too. Seems she was totally controlled by him. It's a minor miracle she managed to escape him before something really bad happened to her. He'd beaten her up rather badly that evening – though we promised her that Harley would know nothing about that, obviously. At least unless it has to come to that down the line. But she's recovering, she'll be fine.'

'And Mum? Has she corroborated everything? If Harley could be spared court, it would mean such a lot.'

The officer smiled. 'I can see you are on the case! But no, not as yet. She's saying she can't remember much of it. Blaming her addictions for her memory lapses. Conveniently.'

Let Me Go

As, I thought, she would. 'That's horrible,' I said. 'I know Harley isn't lying when she says her mum knew. I can't believe she'd persist in denying that.'

Sam shrugged. 'Who knows,' she said, 'but in my job – and yours, I imagine – we come across it all the time. The intention is to re-interview her and then a decision will be made about whether she should face her own charges of neglect – at the very least – but first things first. Let's get Hamzar. Get some justice for those girls. Just terrible what they've been through.' She raised her gaze out towards the conservatory. 'Particularly for that one. Poor mite.'

I agreed. And her mother even *now* wasn't there for her.

Perhaps she never would be. But that was a question for another day. Right now there was really only one way to see it. That it could all have been so, so, much worse.

Chapter 22

As I expected, I got some good-natured ribbing from my husband (and an eye-roll from Tyler, who thought the whole thing was hilarious) but the following day, I made it official. Our twenty-eight days was going to stretch to something more like forty, while a long-term foster family was put in place.

Which was a very different scenario to the one we'd been led to envisage when we'd picked Harley up from that hospital twenty-eight days ago. At that time it had all been so straightforward – well, at least for the first twenty minutes or so. We were going to look after her for four weeks, no longer, before she was returned to her mother.

It was teatime and, as was traditional on certain Saturdays, we were tucking into a huge takeaway pizza. As were Harley and Tyler, but out of earshot over on the sofa, as they were watching something that they absolutely *had* to keep watching, right now, with their pizza, on Netflix. Which, of course they didn't. Even I was savvy enough to know about the pause button. But it was fine. Eating pizza in front of the telly was, well, pretty normal. But a 'normal' that Harley had barely experienced. Which made it very far from normal. It was special. I wouldn't have dreamed of dragging them away from it.

'Well, that was *never* going to happen,' Mike said, picking up his second slab of pepperoni. 'We knew that at the start, love. Well, *I* did, at any rate. Tough though,' he added, 'for her to know that even now everything's come out, her mum still doesn't want her home.'

'She doesn't know,' I told him. 'She just thinks it's because Mum still isn't well enough. And Tessa's let her think that. And I think she's right to. Truth is, everyone thinks that this is the watershed; that Mum will never have either of the girls back. Seems like she wants a fresh start and that doesn't include her daughters.'

'Bloody outrageous if you ask me,' Mike said. 'You'd think she'd want to at least *try* to repair some of the damage, wouldn't you?'

I could see his point, but I was also well aware of the root of that damage – the tool she'd used to self-medicate in the first place. Once a person turns to drugs and alcohol to numb their reality, it complicates everything. The original problems are just swept under the carpet and addiction itself becomes the new problem. It's an extraordinarily difficult cycle to break out of, close to impossible if you don't have support. And definitely impossible if you don't want support, because you don't want to address the problem in the first place.

I suspected Harley's mum was almost certainly in that last camp. And even if she did accept some sort of help, I suspected any progress would be patchy and slow. Could the girls wait to see if things improved? Should they? How many kids' lives were blighted by hoping for the best when, time and again, those hopes were destined to be dashed? No, it was my firm opinion that, now they once again had each other, they'd be better off making a clean break and making new starts for themselves. If Mum came good in time then so be it – the cherry on the cake – but if they started out with no expectations on that front, they wouldn't have to deal with the disappointment. Plus, as Harley had told me, it had always been Millie who'd felt more like her mum. Maybe less so now their respective ages made the age gap shrink a little, but her emotional health, at least for now, and perhaps, to an extent, always, was going to be bound up in her big sister.

I said so to Mike. 'Plus, they both have enough demons of their own to contend with right now. No, I think everyone is exactly where they should be.'

Which, in Harley's case, was with us, but not for very much longer as, a couple of days later, Christine called to say they had approved the foster family who, if everything went well, were going to have her long-term.

'They sound perfect,' she told me. 'Youngish couple, one child of their own – a three-year-old daughter. An interesting one – you wouldn't normally expect such a young family to want to take on a teenager, but the mum, Sian, was in foster care herself as a teenager and credits it with helping her turn her life around after a chaotic and lonely childhood. She wants to give back. Isn't that lovely?' I agreed that it was. 'And even better,' Christine added, 'is that they literally live a fifteen-minute walk away from the supported lodgings Millie's going to be moving into. And it's just a ten-minute walk the other way to the local high school.'

'That's incredible,' I said, because it was. But perhaps not so incredible – perhaps just the fates tipping the scales. It was high time this young girl, who had been through so much, had them work in her favour.

'But we mustn't get ahead of ourselves,' Christine reminded me. 'They've first got to meet and be mutually happy. How does Harley feel about dogs, by the way? They have two rather large ones.'

'OMG, I *love* dogs!' Harley squealed when I relayed this question to her later. 'I mean *really*. My dad used to have a dog. I don't really remember her, because I was still only little when she died, but Millie does. She was a German shepherd, called Softail. I still have a picture of him with her.'

'Softail? Because she had one?'

She shook her head. 'It's one of the Harley-Davidson motorbikes. They make lots of different ones.'

'But there'll only be one Harley.' I smiled at her. 'Well, for me, anyway. I'm going to miss you, you know.'

She looked serious then. 'I'm going to miss you as well. So much. I'm so sorry I made everything so difficult for everyone.'

'Oh, go on with you!'

'You don't have to pretend,' she said. 'I know I've been a royal pain in the bum.'

'*Stop* it,' I chided. 'Compared to some we've had here, let me tell you, you've been an absolute piece of cake.'

Harley grinned. 'You must like some pretty horrible cakes then.' She put a finger to her chin. 'Hmm ... what sort of cake would I be? A sweet strawberry shortcake? A sour lemon drizzle?'

'A blueberry muffin,' I decided. 'Both bitter and sweet. But anyway, enough with the patisserie comparisons. I need to get back to my paperwork so we can sort out this meeting with Mrs and Mrs Moore. Tell you what, how about you go make us some sandwiches for lunch so I can get on with this?'

As I sat and typed an email to the prospective new foster carers, I could hear Harley humming to herself as she pottered in the kitchen. Such a simple thing, a hum. But what a huge amount it meant. Unhappy people, in my experience, never hummed.

Not that I was naïve. Happiness was, of course, relative. There was so much hurt still inside her that perfect happiness would be elusive. Memories would ambush her at unexpected moments, sometimes, I didn't doubt, with the power of a tsunami. And the time would also come (God willing, anyway) when she'd have to find a way to put the horrors of the past into a box, if she was to successfully navigate romantic relationships, something I knew would never be easy. But the weight she had carried for so long had been lifted, and for now, in the moment, she was humming to herself happily. And, for now, being happy in the moment was enough. As she should be. She had gone from having no reason to want to live to having everything to live for. A shot at a happy ending, and for now that was sufficient too.

And happy endings came in all shapes and sizes. As a foster carer, the gold standard was, for me, pretty obvious – a child going home, happily, to their natural parents. But that wasn't going to happen here, as was sadly all too common. With all the will in the world, I couldn't make a mother want her child.

So, Harley's happy ending would be different. Another home to move on to, with strangers she had yet to meet, and new experiences to be had – a future she had not perhaps envisaged. I wasn't sure I'd have had the strength to do it. But Harley was still a child and children never ceased to amaze me. I marvelled all the time at their ability to adapt – to accept their new reality and move bravely on. No, they often didn't have a choice – not the ones I'd been involved with – but when you thought about their backgrounds, how much they'd already been through, it often seemed to me little short of a miracle.

She's such a lovely girl, I typed, tears now prickling in my eyes, *and we are going to miss her terribly, but I'm sure she will bring you a lot of happiness.*

Because it wasn't just one-way traffic, was it? This whole 'caring' business. For every bit of love and care Harley's new family gave her, I knew she would give an equal or even greater amount back. I smiled to myself, blinked back the tears and recalled what I'd laughingly said to Tessa. Which wasn't true.

You definitely *didn't* do a job like mine for the paperwork.

Epilogue

I heard Zar had been arrested through the fostering grapevine. He had managed to evade capture for three weeks and the initial thoughts were that he had somehow left the country. The reality was that the man was a lot closer to home.

The same uncle whose kebab shop he'd been running for the past year owned three further takeaway outlets around the country and having no idea of the crimes his nephew had committed, had been happy to give him work in another of his outlets; a fresh start after the break-up of his relationship.

He was caught, in the end, quite by chance. He'd been flagged down because he'd had a driver's side light out on his car and the registration number had shown up as flagged on the police database. And when the time came for him to have his day in court, he was found guilty of all the child abuse charges filed against him and sent to jail for a number of years.

Harley and Millie's mum, on the other hand, was never charged with anything. Following a formal assessment of her fitness to testify, it was deemed she lacked capacity and it was felt that little purpose would be served by prosecuting her for anything, as, in many ways, not least because she'd been so incapacitated by her addictions, she was a victim like her daughters.

She was, though, as a condition of charges not being made against her, required by social services to accept counselling, including drug and alcohol sessions, which were apparently reasonably successful. Harley was not returned to her, however. Though she apparently expressed regret, and a desire to be reunited with her daughters when she was better, neither Millie nor Harley, by that time, were keen – and after all the progress that had been achieved in the intervening months, Millie's wonderful foster parents weren't either. They were happy to support Harley in any reconciliation, obviously, but it was clear that, unless she was keen for that to happen, it might be best to let sleeping dogs lie. So, though neither girl ruled out some sort of relationship with their mother in the future, at the time of writing, that's how things remain.

Which is as good a reminder – as if anyone ever needed reminding – that the future isn't promised; that life can change in a moment. That we should hug and cherish everyone close to us. Though I obviously never knew him, I often wonder how the lives of all of them might have panned out had Harley's dad not been knocked off his beloved motorbike. Had his young wife not been quite so young when she'd been widowed. Had her own parents not, as I learned later, rebuffed all attempts by her and her young husband to reconcile their differences. Of all the characters in this sad, harrowing tale, it's perhaps Harley's mum's parents who perplex me the most. It's a parent's prerogative to disapprove of their children's choices, obviously. It's a parent's duty – to my mind – to keep a sense of perspective too. To support and accept their children, however much the choices they make are out of step with the imaginary futures they might have planned for them. To be fair, they probably never anticipated how much their rejection of their teenage daughter impacted on so many lives, and how adversely. Still, it's food for thought, isn't it? To know that humans can and do make such harsh decisions. If only, when her husband died, they hadn't been quite so estranged that Harley's mum couldn't face trying again with them.

As for the girls themselves, well, I'm happy to report they are both well, and, dare I risk saying it, thriving. Having settled in so well with her new foster carers, the child Harley was perhaps destined to be, had life not dealt her such a bad hand, emerged like a butterfly from a pupa. She still has a lot to process, and perhaps the scars of her abuse by Zar will never fully heal, but she is in a supportive environment, cared for by people who want only what's best for her. They have now applied for her to stay with them till she turns eighteen, and possibly longer, as she is keen to stay in full-time education. She's obviously missed a lot of school but has settled well into her new one and, now she isn't also struggling with an unhappy and chaotic home life, she's apparently doing really well.

The icing on the cake for Harley, of course, is that she's been reunited with Millie, who moved out of the supported lodgings she was placed in initially, and, with the help of social services, found a flat to rent which is also close to where Harley and her foster family live. Since we last saw her, she's been to college to gain a counselling qualification and is now working for a charity that supports abused women.

As for us Watsons, life calmed down for a bit. Well, as much as it could do with a new baby in the family and Nanna committed to help with the childcare.

And Kieron was right: the hot-water bottle came in very handy.

A note on twenty-eight-day placements

I thought it was worth saying a little more about the rise of the twenty-eight-day placement. As you'll already have gathered from reading Harley's story, I have a bit of an issue (to say the least!) with their increasing use. Also known as an emergency placement, for obvious reasons, they can be used with very little notice – normally just a few hours – when there is some kind of crisis involved. A distraught parent, for example, who is at the end of their tether, and is demanding their child be taken away. In an instance such as this, as was the case with Harley's mother, the service will assess the crisis to better understand the bigger picture, and if it's deemed that the child would be at risk unless put in a safe environment, a foster family will be sought immediately.

Longstanding readers will know that Mike and I already take on children with little notice as a matter of course, and often do so in emergency situations, with all the complications that entails. So why, you might wonder, is this any different? After all, being thrown in at the deep end is something we've come to accept is an inevitable part of our kind of fostering. And you'd be right, because it is.

The difference here, however, is that it's a bit like taking on a job without a job spec. The very nature of it is that it's not only strictly time limited (that's a legal requirement) but also that you really are just expected to provide bed and board, till the child is returned home (the ideal situation, obviously), or a long-term foster family is found and properly matched to them.

We've taken in children for both extremely short and extremely long periods, but always with a specific role to play. As specialist carers, we take children who are already in care and, because of particularly challenging behaviours, perhaps, have not managed to settle into their foster homes. We've had children who've only just entered the care system but who are so troubled that they just can't cope with most family situations. We've also had children for whom the prospect of a 'forever' foster family is never going to be much more than a dream; in such cases our role is to do whatever we can to help a child become socialised enough, and, as far as possible, in control of their destructive, and self-destructive, impulses so that they can at least function day-to-day. And in all but the most extreme cases, the intense work we do is geared towards them settling in a new long-term home.

With the twenty-eight-day placement, however, we have no defined positive role – at least as I see it. We are just expected to facilitate what's being done by other professionals, as they work with both child and family to get them home again, perhaps with support put in place.

Which is fine as an idea but, increasingly, not what happens in practice. In Harley's case, for example, her mother didn't want to engage with any services. Her child had, in her opinion, become a liability, and she felt better off on her own. And with Harley, too, because she had felt so let down by her mother, there was little desire to try and build any bridges. In which case (again, this is just my opinion), a full care order would have been the more productive option, as it would have drawn a line and enabled all concerned to adapt more quickly to the new reality, and that's apart from the other inherent problem with such placements – that everyone is going into them blind. There are no assessments made, and no pre-placement meetings either, so everyone ends up fumbling around in the dark, which isn't a nice place for foster carers (by their nature, people who are motivated to love and to nurture, to get to know the child and build up their trust) to find themselves in.

There is, of course, a pool of foster families who are both committed to and trained in these types of place-ment, just as there are those who specialise in and are dedicated to short-term and/or respite care. (Annie and Oscar, the little ones we looked after just before having Harley, are an example of children who required just that – a safe place to stay before returning to their parents.) The problem is – and it always seems to come down to this nowadays – that resources and funding are increasingly scarce, so all foster carers are now expected to do this kind of work.

Again, no foster carer is going to refuse to take a child in if they desperately need a home, but because of a lack of funding in the community coupled with cuts in social services, more and more children are coming into the system. More families are in crisis, and end up calling and relying on a service that is already stretched almost to breaking point, and the children of these families require urgent attention. This, I believe, is what's behind the twenty-eight-day placement being used more frequently than perhaps it should be. And also the reason for so many of the children brought into the system on that basis not really being suited to such a regime.

I was pretty adamant that, after Harley, we didn't want to do any more twenty-eight-day placements, yet following her departure, we went on to do four more. Each of them was as heartbreaking as the others, in their different ways, and in all cases definitely not the type of child that only required bed and board and a car available so they could be chauffeured to meetings. Two of them were children that we had to pick up from the very same psychiatric hospital that Harley had been in, one was a transgender child on the verge of suicide and the fourth was a sibling placement – two little tots who were waiting to be adopted.

Again, if you are a regular reader, you will know how emotionally exhausting this is; our family simply couldn't just 'house' these kids and not be affected by them. It was devastating for me to do these placements and then just let go. I'd go so far as to say it was too awful for words. We came into fostering to roll our sleeves up and try to make a difference, to build a relationship with a child and help *them* build as well – their trust, their resilience, their control, their self-esteem. And though some were always going to be more able to do that than others, that sense of making progress was, and always will be, a key part of what we love about what we do.

So I think it's clear – I don't like twenty-eight-day placements! That said, at the time of writing, despite telling Christine we don't want to, I fully expect Mike and I to be doing more. Let's just keep our fingers crossed that something improves. Oh, and if you're thinking about fostering, don't let this put you off. Despite my gripes, it's still the most rewarding thing we've ever done, and there's life in this grumpy old dog yet!

If any of the issues in this book affected you there are organisations available to help.

NHS Choices
www.nhs.uk/conditions/suicide/

The Samaritans
samaritans.org

Samaritans is available round the clock, every single day of the year. They provide a safe place for anyone struggling to cope. Please call 116 123, email jo@samaritans.org, or visit www.samaritans.org to find details of your nearest branch.

Shout
giveusashout.org

Shout is the UK's first free 24/7 text service for anyone in crisis anytime, anywhere. It's a place to go if you're struggling to cope and you need immediate help. Text Shout to 85258.

CASEY WATSON

One woman determined to
make a difference.

Read Casey's poignant
memoirs and be inspired.

NOWHERE TO GO

Eleven-year-old Tyler has stabbed his stepmother and has nowhere to go

With his birth mother dead and a father who doesn't want him, what can be done to stop his young life spiralling out of control?

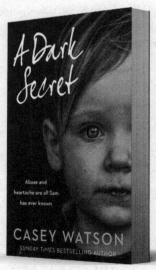

A DARK SECRET

A troubled nine-year-old with a violent streak, Sam's relentless bullying sees even his siblings beg not to be placed with him

When Casey delves into Sam's past she uncovers something far darker than she had imagined.

A BOY WITHOUT HOPE

A history of abuse and neglect has left Miller destined for life's scrap heap

Miller's destructive behaviour will push Casey to her limits, but she is determined to help him overcome his demons and give him hope.

GROOMED

Keeley is urgently rehomed with Casey after accusing her foster father of abuse

It's Casey's job to keep Keeley safe, but can she protect this strong-willed teen from the dangers online?

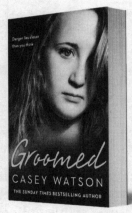

THE SILENT WITNESS

Bella's father is on a ventilator, fighting for his life, while her mother is currently on remand in prison, charged with his attempted murder

Bella is the only witness.

RUNAWAY GIRL

Adrianna arrives on Casey's doorstep with no possessions, no English and no explanation

It will be a few weeks before Casey starts getting the shocking answers to her questions . . .

MUMMY'S LITTLE SOLDIER

Leo isn't a bad lad, but his frequent absences from school mean he's on the brink of permanent exclusion

Leo is clearly hiding something, and Casey knows that if he is to have any kind of future, it's up to her to find out the truth.

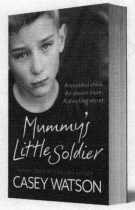

SKIN DEEP

Flip is being raised by her alcoholic mother, and comes to Casey after a fire at their home

Flip has Foetal Alcohol Syndrome (FAS), but it soon turns out that this is just the tip of the iceberg . . .

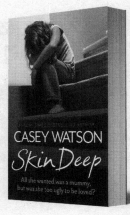

A STOLEN CHILDHOOD

Kiara appears tired and distressed, and the school wants Casey to take her under her wing for a while

On the surface, everything points to a child who is upset that her parents have separated. The horrific truth, however, shocks Casey to the core.

THE GIRL WITHOUT A VOICE

What is the secret behind Imogen's silence?

Discover the shocking and devastating past of a child with severe behavioural problems.

A LAST KISS FOR MUMMY

A teenage mother and baby in need of a loving home

At fourteen, Emma is just a child herself – and one who's never been properly mothered.

BREAKING THE SILENCE

Two boys with an unlikely bond

With Georgie and Jenson, Casey is facing her toughest test yet.

MUMMY'S LITTLE HELPER

A young girl secretly caring for her mother

Abigail has been dealing with pressures no child should face. Casey has the difficult challenge of helping her to learn to let go.

TOO HURT TO STAY

Branded 'vicious and evil', eight-year-old Spencer asks to be taken into care

Casey and her family are disgusted: kids aren't born evil. Despite the challenges Spencer brings, they are determined to help him find a loving home.

LITTLE PRISONERS

Abused siblings who do not know
what it means to be loved

With new-found security and trust,
Casey helps Ashton and Olivia to
rebuild their lives.

CRYING FOR HELP

A damaged girl haunted
by her past

Sophia pushes Casey to the limits,
threatening the safety of the whole
family. Can Casey make a
difference in time?

THE BOY NO ONE
LOVED

Five-year-old Justin was
desperate and helpless

Six years after being taken into care,
Justin has had 20 failed placements. Casey
and her family are his last hope.

TITLES AVAILABLE AS E-BOOK ONLY

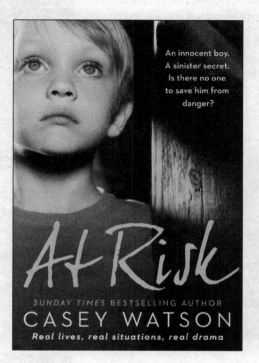

AT RISK

Adam is brought to Casey while his mum recovers in hospital – just for a few days

But a chance discovery reveals that Casey has stumbled upon something altogether more sinister . . .

THE LITTLE PRINCESS

Six-year-old Darby is naturally distressed at being removed from her parents just before Christmas

And when the shocking and sickening reason is revealed, a Happy New Year seems an impossible dream as well . . .

DADDY'S BOY

Paulie, just five, is a boy out of control – or is he just misunderstood?

The plan for Paulie is simple: get him back home with his family. But perhaps 'home' isn't the best place for him . . .

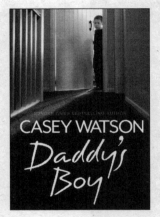

THE WILD CHILD

Angry and hurting, eight-year-old Connor is from a broken home

As streetwise as they come, he's determined to cause trouble. But Casey is convinced there is a frightened child beneath the swagger.

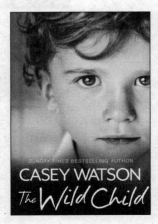

NO PLACE FOR NATHAN

Nathan has a sometime alter ego called Jenny who is the only one who knows the secrets of his disturbed past

But where is Jenny when she is most needed?

SCARLETT'S SECRET

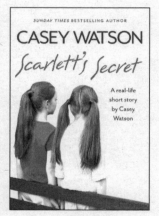

Jade and Scarlett, seventeen-year-old twins, share a terrible secret

Can Casey help them come to terms with the truth and rediscover their sibling connection?

JUST A BOY

Cameron is a sweet boy who seems happy in his skin – making him rather different from most of the other children Casey has cared for

But what happens when Cameron disappears? Will Casey's worst fears be realised?

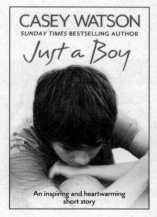

FEEL HEART.
FEEL HOPE.
READ CASEY.

Discover more about Casey Watson.
Visit www.caseywatson.co.uk

Find Casey Watson on **f** & 🐦

MOVING
Memoirs

Stories of hope, courage and
the power of love . . .

Sign up to the Moving Memoirs email and you'll
be the first to hear about new books, discounts,
and get sneak previews from your
favourite authors!

Sign up at

www.moving-memoirs.com